The Book of
BARNSTAPLE

AVRIL STONE

NÉE BARTHRAM

HALSGROVE

First published in Great Britain in 2002
Reprinted 2003. Revised and reprinted 2012

> *This book is dedicated to my father Alf Barthram*
> *who had a gift for telling a good story better*
> *than anyone I know.*

Frontispiece photograph: *The Poultry and Caged Bird Show*
in the Pannier Market, c.1920.

British Library Cataloguing-in-Publication Data
A CIP record for this title is available from the British Library

ISBN 978 0 85704 176 0

HALSGROVE
Halsgrove House,
Ryelands Business Park,
Bagley Road, Wellington, Somerset TA21 9PZ
Tel: 01823 653777   Fax: 01823 216796
email: sales@halsgrove.com

Part of the Halsgrove group of companies
Information on all Halsgrove titles is available at: www.halsgrove.com

Printed and bound in China by Everbest Printing Ltd

CONTENTS

PREFACE

Ten years have passed since *Barnstaple – Memories of a Coastal Market Town* was first published, followed by Volume II *From Coronation to Millennium* in 2003.

Author Avril Stone

When I was asked to write an update as a postscript for this Diamond Jubilee issue I was pleased to accept but somewhat daunted as I'd spent most of the intervening years on the West Coast of Scotland living out a dream with my husband Eric. We often travelled home to Barnstaple to visit our family and of course kept up with events through local newspapers and South West television.

When we moved north the West Country had been devastated by foot and mouth disease. The farming community was in despair and the future looked bleak for this area. The cattle market in the centre of the town had closed leading, some people felt, to the slow death of the centuries old tradition of the country coming to town on a Friday, with the high impact that would have on the Pannier Market and town centre shops. Some will still say that those fears have been borne out.

Since returning to live in Barnstaple I have looked and listened to what local people and visitors have to say about the town and I've hopefully found that Barumites can deal with adversity with their well respected kindness, generosity and sense of humour.

AVRIL STONE, 2012

ACKNOWLEDGEMENTS

Credits for the main part of this book can be found in the first issue. For this new edition I must acknowledge the help, support and advice that I receive from my husband Eric and my dearest friend Jean Woodhams (who also works wonders with her magic red subbing pen!).

I also thank all those people who have willingly given me their thoughts and opinions about Barnstaple at the turn of this century. For help with news events and photographs a very big thank-you to the staff of the *North Devon Journal* and especially its Editor, Chloe Hubbard (our own local girl made good!).

My gratitude to Town Centre Manager Craig Bulley and his assistant Sue Rawle, to Cllr and Mayor 2010-12 Ian Roome, Town Clerk Ann Jenkins and her assistant, Julie Parker, and Cllr Simon Harvey, also, Claire Thompson and Sarah Anderson of the Queen's Theatre Trust, Jonathan Ellwood and Mike Beagley. And last but by no means least to farming sage Albert Beer for taking me down memory lane.

REFERENCES

Written Sources Used as Reference.

Books:
Guide to Barnstaple Guildhall by Barnstaple Town Council.
Postcard Views of North Devon, Volume IV by Tom Bartlett.
Barnstaple Yesterday by Julia and Jonathan Baxter.
North Devon Art Pottery by Audrey Edgeler and John Edgeler.
Around Barnstaple by Francis Frith.
Barnstaple's Vanished Lace Industry by Peter Christie and Deborah Gahan.
Memorials of Barnstaple by Joseph Besly Gribble.
Dr Richard Harper of Barnstaple by Margery Harper.
A Brief History of Rackfield House by Margery Harper.
Barnstaple Town on the Taw by Lois Lamplugh.
The Show Goes On by Sandra Paxford.
Strong's Industries of North Devon by H.W. Strong.
Us Be Goin to Barnstaple Fair by Maureen E. Wood.

Barnstaple Heritage Booklets:
Barnstaple's Heritage Time-Line by J.C. Andrews.
Shipbuilding at Barnstaple by M.C. Taylor.
Thomas Benson by M.C. Taylor.

Other Resources:
1950 Our Centenary Year, Rawle, Gammon & Baker booklet.
Barnstaple and District Official Guidebooks.
Barnstaple Swimming Club Diamond Jubilee 1992 booklet.
Brochure of Barnstaple Grammar School 1915.
The Borough of a Thousand Years 930–1930. Barnstaple Millenary Official Brochure.
North Devon Advertiser.
North Devon Journal Herald.
Western Morning News.

Chapter One

EARLY HISTORY

R.L. Knight photograph of sketch of Barnstaple Quay (artist unknown).

Standing on any hilltop overlooking Barnstaple you will see this North Devon town nestling in a bowl at the head of the River Taw estuary. It is easy to understand why a settlement began here over 1,000 years ago. There is shelter from the surrounding hills, fresh water from the Rivers Yeo and Taw, and the sea that twice daily washes in from Barnstaple Bay a few miles away.

During the summer months North Devon is a throng of bustling holiday-makers who come to enjoy the miles of sandy beaches, surf the Atlantic rollers or explore the wild beauty of Exmoor. Barnstaple is the region's principal town and today is the centre of commercial and retail enterprise, medical facilities, education, sports, leisure and tourism. Most visitors find themselves at some time during their holiday sojourn sampling the sights and sounds of this ancient market town, with its hidden cobbled lanes and courtyards, famous Pannier

Market and its international prize-winning floral decorations.

This book concentrates on memories of life in Barnstaple from the people who have lived and worked in the town during the twentieth century. However, we begin with a brief history of the first 1,000 years of this ancient borough.

The name Barnstaple has had many variations before arriving at the present spelling. To the ancient Britons it was Abertawe, 'standing on the mouth of the River Taw'. The Saxons changed this to Beardestaple: the staple or market of Bearda. But through the ages one name could always find this town. Barnstaple was, and still is, commonly known as Barum, from the Latin *Barumensis*.

Since Saxon times Barnstaple has been the major influence of the north of the county. Alfred the Great made Pilton a 'Burgh' (a borough). His grandson Athelstan found that Barnstaple was ideally situated for a fortified military installation, so he had a wall and gates built around the town. For hundreds of years it was thought that in AD930 Athelstan had granted the town a charter, making it the oldest borough in England. This has since been disputed, but it did not stop the elders of the town celebrating its millenary in 1930. A point that is not the subject of controversy, however, is that Athelstan established a mint in the town.

The Domesday Book of 1086 shows there was a sizable settlement here. This document states that:

The King has 40 burgesses within the borough and 9 without, and they pay 40 shillings by weight to the King and 20 shillings by tale to the Bishop of Countances.

Barnstaple even had its own MP for almost 600 years! The first was elected in 1295 to the new Model Parliament of Edward I and the last was elected in 1885, when the parliamentary divisions were changed.

Situated as it is on the estuary, with easy access to the Bristol Channel and surrounded by agricultural land, the town naturally has its history connected with both seafaring and farming. From the early-thirteenth century it was an important port, not only for ships of warfare but also for trading and shipbuilding. Pilgrimage ships also sailed from Barnstaple: for example, in 1434 the 40-ton single-masted *Nicholas*, with 400 pilgrims on board, set sail for the shrine of St James at Compostella in Spain.

In 1588 Barnstaple sent five ships to fight the Armada. Following the defeat of the Spanish many of the prisoners were kept on Lundy Island after first being brought to Barnstaple and held at the Quay Hall. Merchants who had suffered losses at the hands of the Spanish were given licences to take reprisal voyages and to seize goods and merchandise from the enemy. At least 15 shipowners in the town were given these 'letters of marque' and many made their fortunes, returning with gold and other treasures. Pentecost Dodderidge was one such merchant. His 100-ton *Prudence* went on two such voyages during 1590–92.

It was a time of seafaring adventure and the town flourished with the importing and exporting trades. Alongside seafaring went trades such as victualling, rope making, chandlery and candle making. Shipbuilding was a major industry in the town until the end of the First World War.

Barnstaple's other commercial successes were potters, brewers, bakers, lace makers and glovers, dyers and, of course, farmers, especially those who farmed sheep, from which woollen and leather products were made.

Across the country the mid-seventeenth century was a period of unrest which saw three years of civil war and was a difficult time for the people of North Devon. The town of Barnstaple changed from the possession of the Roundheads and Royalists four times! First the Parliamentarians held the town, then in 1643 the Royalists took over. The following year the Roundheads once again took control, but not for long, as the King's men recaptured the town. Finally the Roundheads triumphed.

In 1646 the Plague was brought to the town in a bundle of clothes found in the river by four brothers who were fishing from the banks of the Taw, where

Below: *Square-rigged* Merchantman *alongside Barnstaple Quay, c.1870.*

· BARNSTAPLE DOCKS, QUEEN ANNE'S WALK & THE OLD STAR INN ·

· THE LONG BRIDGE & LIME KILN ·

Right: *Sketch of the North Gate prior to 1840.*

Below: *Pilton Bridge and Pilton Quay, c.1900.*

THE NORTH GATE

· THE OLD MUSIC HALL, LATER THE ALBERT HALL · (destroyed)

These sketches and those opposite were drawn by Jonathan Lomas.

· MONKEY OR CYPRUS ISLAND & POND ·

the leisure centre stands at the time of writing. John, Joseph, Richard and Thomas Ley all died and the epidemic spread throughout the town. The boys' mother planted seven elm trees in their memory along the bank where they had been fishing. The area became known as Seven Brethren Bank. The trees were removed in 1852 to make way for the railway.

The many changes and developments in the town during the nineteenth century included the introduction of lace making and glove factories, iron founding and cabinet makers. Shipbuilding continued and Westacott's yard, which had been situated at the end of Litchdon Street on the River Taw, moved to the higher side of Long Bridge to enable it to build larger boats. However, by the end of the century all shipyards in the borough had closed.

The first issue of the *North Devon Journal* was printed in 1824, and 1826 saw the opening of the North Devon Infirmary. In 1829 a swing-bridge was built over the River Yeo at Rolle Quay. Previously, those travelling to Braunton had to make their way around Yeo Vale and Pilton.

A private water company started operations in 1830. Unfiltered water was taken twice a week from the River Yeo and stored in reservoirs before being pumped to customers. Most people, however, continued to be supplied from private wells or by water merchants who drew water from the Yeo on Saturdays and sold it around the streets on Mondays.

The railway arrived in 1854 and with it a multitude of changes. To start with, Barnstaple advanced its clocks by 15 minutes to take on London time. Mail, newspapers and other commodities, including cattle and sheep, were now easily transported. And, of course, this opened up the countryside to the holiday-maker.

In 1879 William Frederick Rock, a London printer who originated from Barnstaple, had a park built for the townspeople on land where there once stood an old factory, cottages, timber and brickyards, claypits and limekilns. It was named Rock Park after its benefactor. Rock also bought a large private house on the town end of Long Bridge and donated it as an Athenaeum for the inhabitants of the town.

❧ *Town Landmarks* ❧

Left: *North Devon Infirmary, c.1920.*

Right: *The Square, c.1965.*

Below: *Entrance to Rock Park on Taw Vale. The Rock Monument was erected to the benefactor of the park, W.F. Rock.*

Chapter Two

HISTORICAL TOUR OF THE TOWN

A tranquil scene in Newport where today there is a busy crossroads, c.1900.

We will start our journey on the eastern end of the town at Newport. The name may have come from a port established on the River Taw where another river, called Coney Gut, enters it. In the distant past Newport was separated from Barnstaple by Coney Gut and wide marshland and had to be reached from the main town by looping north and coming in at the top end of Newport through St John's Lane. As late as 1835 it was still a separate borough with its own mayor. It had many shops – bakers, butchers, dairies and general stores, and also trades, including building, carpentry, undertaking and even gloving.

After the marshland was reclaimed the residents of Newport were able to enjoy a less circuitous walk into the town, or a ride on the regular horse-drawn carriage services, later succeeded by motorised ones.

In 1822 there was an iron foundry where Parkside Garage stands at the time of writing. It was

run by Thomas Willshire and employed 50 men. A former apprentice, Thomas Lake, and his brother Edwin went on to open their own foundry in Victoria Road and then another in a large garden behind Number 61 Newport Road, which was bought with the help of the dowry of Tom's wife Hannah, a local baker's daughter. The years saw the Wilshere foundry describing a very varied history. First it became Oliver's Cabinet Works, which showed just how wide the town's trade links were with the outside world. Barnstaple was no backwater! Oliver's made not only furniture but fine marquetry for churches, ships and railways in many countries, especially for the Indian railways.

The old foundry site was later home to the John Gay Theatre, which was built in 1930, and then to an auto firm. The theatre survived a mere 20 or so years and was sold in 1951 to Albert Symons, along with West Regional Autos. Albert's

Above: *Thomas Willshire's iron foundry at the bottom of Newport Road.*

Above: *Approaching the Square from Taw Vale, c.1900.*

Right: *The Imperial Hotel, c.1900.*

daughter, Lorna Ward, remembers her grandmother setting to and turning the red stage curtains into eiderdowns for the family's beds (and handsome ones they were too!).

Approaching the town along Taw Vale we reach Rock Park, which, since it was gifted by Barnstaple's great benefactor William Rock, has seen many major celebrations, from royal anniversary tea parties to the annual carnival procession.

Taw Vale itself did not exist before the late 1800s. The road, with its wide pavement alongside the river and eye-catching floral decorations in the summer, formed part of the rear gardens of houses in Litchdon Street – once the main road from the town through to Newport and on to Exeter and Taunton.

The Imperial Hotel stands near the entrance to the Square; this was opened in 1898 from what was once a private house.

Above: *The Square with horse-drawn taxis, c.1910.*
Photograph R.L. Knight.

Above: *The Square, c.1920. The building on the far left, Albert Place, was Barnstaple's prison until 1874.*
Photograph R.L. Knight.

The Long Bridge.
Courtesy Bath Photographic.

The Square

In 1732 the Square was reclaimed from marshy wasteland. The Albert Memorial Clock was built in 1862 by public subscription. Old cottages were demolished at the end of the bridge ten years later and a large private house was built. This was purchased by William Rock and became the Athenaeum, which today houses the North Devon Museum. Where horse-drawn cabs once stood patiently for hire and pedestrians peacefully ambled across this ornamental public amenity there is now a whirlpool of traffic.

Long Bridge

The Long Bridge has spanned the River Taw since Norman times. In 1273 Henry de Tracey, Lord of Barnstaple, had a stone bridge built. This had a wooden drawbridge at the town end and a toll had to be paid to gain admittance. It was also an effective way of keeping undesirables out!

In 1589 the drawbridge was removed and three stone arches were built in its place. These became known as the Maiden Arches. Over the years the bridge has been widened and strengthened several times.

❧ The Strand ❧

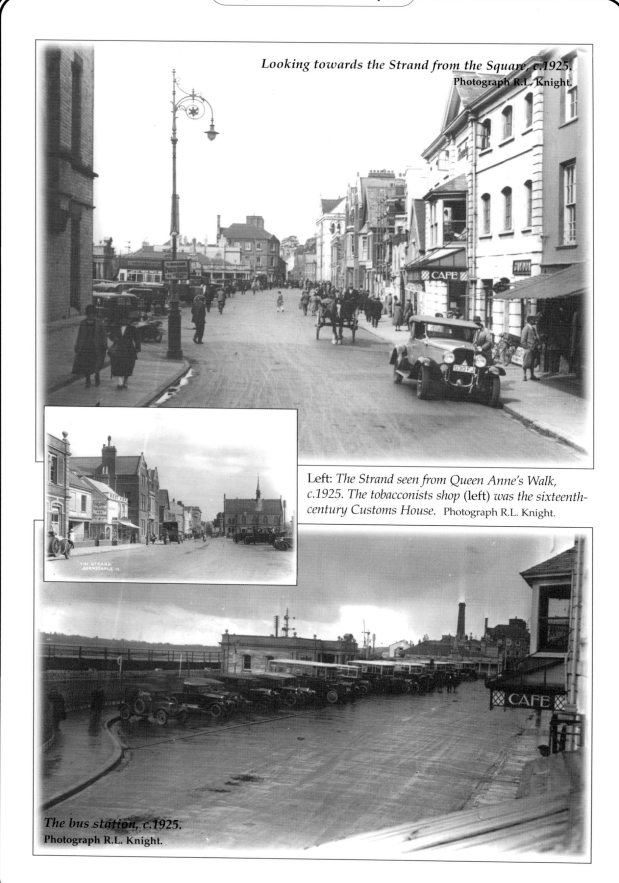

Looking towards the Strand from the Square, c.1925.
Photograph R.L. Knight.

Left: *The Strand seen from Queen Anne's Walk, c.1925. The tobacconists shop (left) was the sixteenth-century Customs House.* Photograph R.L. Knight.

The bus station, c.1925.
Photograph R.L. Knight.

The Strand

In the 1300s the first known guildhall stood at the entrance to Maiden Street, where Bridge Buildings stand at the time of writing. The Strand is now a thoroughfare for traffic and people enjoy the walk along the riverside promenade, but here is Barnstaple's link with its long maritime history. This was the quay and was therefore the business heart of the town. Ships came home to port here, where the Customs House, the Fish Shambles and bonded warehouses were also located. The Quay Hall, the mercantile centre where a cloth market was held in the 1400s, stood next to the West Gate and the entrance to Cross Street. The town lock-up was also here.

Being a busy port it goes without saying that there were numerous public houses and hotels in the vicinity. To name a few there was the Star Inn, Queen Anne's Temperance Hotel, the Angel Hotel (later to become the Regal Cinema) and the Bell Hotel, which was first named the Bellerophon after a warship during the Napoleonic War.

Before the quay wall was built the river probably reached the buildings on the far side of the Strand. Michael Bromley informed me that in 1924 his father, who already owned a bakery and tearooms in the High Street, obtained a property on the Strand. It had previously been Andrews Coal Merchants. During excavations to build a ballroom adjoining the tearooms the builders uncovered a mooring post.

Many people will remember Bromley's Tearooms with the waitresses in their black uniform dresses, with pristine white aprons, and the grand occasions, weddings, balls and dances. Taxis would draw up to the main entrance on the Strand and men in their dinner suits and ladies in long evening gowns would sweep in through the doors with doormen at the ready. How grand I felt when I went to my first dance there. So grown up, so chic! Alas, those days of grandeur have disappeared. However, so have the yards of prickly net petticoats and winklepicker shoes, whose passing are not to be mourned!

Equally well known was Bromley's Snack Bar on the Strand where you perched on high stools with red leather seats at the counter which ran around the room. Piping hot tea or coffee and snacks could be bought while you waited for your bus, which you could conveniently see arrive across the road at the bus station. The Snack Bar was frequented by bus drivers and conductors and I recall there always appeared to be a light-hearted atmosphere about the place. In 1974 Bromley's was sold and became Chequers Night Club and later, under different ownership, was turned into another club called Zenaxis. Unfortunately, the grandeur of the building has gone, but it is not forgotten by local residents.

Above: *Mrs Bromley and waitresses.* Left to right: *Mrs Fry, Mrs King, Mrs Bromley and Mrs Parminter.*

Above: *Bromley's entrance on the Strand, c.1925.*
Photograph R.L. Knight.

Theatre Lane is a narrow thoroughfare that runs through from the Strand to the High Street between what was the Regal Cinema and Bromley's Snack Bar. It was no doubt thus named because until 1828 Shakespeares Theatre was located here. This closed when the Theatre Royal opened in Boutport Street.

The riverfront is now an attractive promenade with a water feature, flowerbeds and mosaics, providing a haven for the delight of visitors and residents alike. In the past it was from here that ships left to trade with near and far continents and where five men o' war left for the Armada. Until 1873 the Fish Shambles stood here but had to be demolished to make way for the Quay railway station. This in turn had to be moved further along the waterfront when the Lynton railway was built in 1898. The Town Station still stands on North Walk and is used by Pathfields School.

The bus station was built on the Strand in 1922 and served the community well from the days of charabancs to coaches and buses bringing country folk to town on Fridays and carrying holiday-makers at weekends to catch onward buses to coastal destinations. The new millennium saw a new bus station on a site at Queen Street. The original bus station building is now a riverfront café.

The Strand

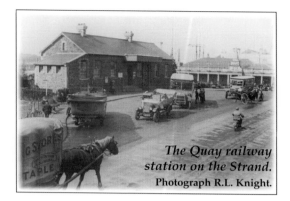

The Quay railway station on the Strand.
Photograph R.L. Knight.

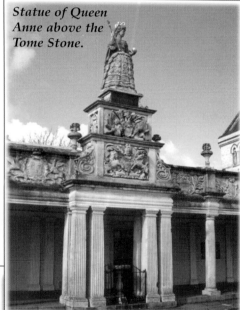

Statue of Queen Anne above the Tome Stone.

Top right: *Water feature on the Strand 2002. Queen Anne's Walk is in the background with the café which was once the bus station on the left.*

Above: *View taken from Long Bridge of the railway bridge to the Quay station, c.1900. Note the old buildings along the waterfront which became the bus station in 1922.*

The Strand, c.1960.

Charabancs preparing for an outing on the Strand, c.1925.

Queen Anne's Walk is still an impressive building and houses the Heritage Centre. It dates back to 1709 when the merchants who used the quayside for their trading decided to improve it by having it roofed. It had been known as Merchants Walk but after Robert Rolle of Stevenstone erected a statue of Queen Anne on the roof it became known by its present name. At its centre is the Tome Stone, over which merchants struck their deals.

Cross Street

Until 1852 the entrance into Cross Street from the Strand was fronted by the town's West Gate. In the 1300s this was known as Crokke Street, which later became Cross – most probably because the town's High Cross stood at its High Street end.

In this street in 1610 the successful merchant, Pentecost Dodderidge, had a town house built. This was demolished in 1910 to enlarge the Post Office building. Thankfully some of the interior panelling was rescued and today can be seen in the aptly named Dodderidge Room in the present Guildhall. Opposite this new Post Office stood the bank owned by Fox, Fowler & Company. At the time of writing Lloyds Bank stands on the site.

Castle Street & Castle Quay

Castle Street is the road which continues on from the Strand, running around the town centre. Barnstaple's last prison was built here in 1878 on the corner of Castle Street and Holland Street. This building later became the Police Station and today is the offices of the Probation Service. So it has stayed within the long arm of the law ever since it was built.

It also runs parallel with Castle Quay, which until the mid 1960s was a working port. Between road and quay the town's electricity station was built. Coal was brought in by boat to fuel the power station and timber was also landed here.

As mentioned earlier, the Town Station was built at the furthest end of Castle Quay in 1898 to accommodate the Lynton railway line as well as the line to Ilfracombe. This was also very conveniently situated across the road from the Cattle Market.

North Walk

North Walk was once a large piece of marshy wasteland at the mouth of the River Yeo. In 1885 the Borough Architect, R.D. Gould, designed a pleasure park with a lake and island as a local amenity. Unfortunately this was short-lived, as it had to be demolished to make way for the Lynton railway line.

The annual fair, which has visited the town since time immemorial, moved its pitch from the Square to North Walk in 1877. This meant that the horse fair, held in North Walk on the second day of the fair week, now had to be moved to the Strand. The rest of the year this area of land had been little used other than as a car park or for the occasional event.

Castle Green with its Castle Mound is the small pleasant park opposite the Civic Centre, on a site which was home to a castle in Saxon times. Later, a private house was built here. The Town Council bought this building in 1926 and used it to house their offices. My memories of this building are scarce as I only ventured in here once when I was five years

Above: *Fox, Fowler & Company cheque, 1917.*

Right: *View from North Walk towards Castle Street with flock of sheep emerging from the Cattle Market. The Town Station is on the right.*
Photograph R.L. Knight.

North Walk

Left: *Aerial view of North Walk before the Civic Centre was built in 1970.*

Right: *Cypress Island on ground where today stands the Civic Centre. Note the tree-lined walk on the right of the picture – this was North Walk.*
Photograph R.L. Knight.

Left: *The fair along North Walk.*

Above: *The Council offices on Castle Green. Designed by W.C. Oliver, the building was demolished in 1976.*

Left: *Brunswick Wharf, belonging to builder and timber merchant, William Gould.*

Right: *Mermaid Cross, c.1950. North Walk on the right was closed on this occasion for the fair.*

Left: *North Gate House, the home of William Gould, at the entrance to Rolle Bridge.*

old and had been chosen as a May Queen attendant, but I can still recall the smell of beeswax polish on the dark wood-panelled walls and highly polished wooden floors. This building was demolished in 1976, much to the dismay of many townsfolk.

Thomas Brannam worked at Rendell's Pottery in Potters Lane, which then ran from North Walk alongside Castle Green.

Tuly Street (once Tooley Street) runs from North Walk back into the town centre and the Cattle Market. Where the library stands today was once the borough poorhouse. In the early 1800s the Master of this establishment was the uncle of the famous landscape painter J.M.W. Turner. In 1811 Turner visited his uncle in Barnstaple whilst on a tour of Devon to make sketches of rural life.

Near the end of North Walk the Boys Blue Coat School once stood, which was built in 1844 and demolished in 1968. Next door was the corner of the High Street and the Mermaid Inn – later called the North Gate Hotel (*see photograph above, right*).

Brunswick Wharf, where boats discharged their cargoes of sand and gravel into Gould's builders yard, was on the opposite side of North Walk. Mr Gould's residence, North Gate House, stood between his yard and the end of Rolle Bridge. Until it closed in 1935, the Lynton railway crossed the road by Rolle Bridge. On the Pilton side of the bridge stood Town Mills, a corn-mill with a large water-wheel, constantly fed by the leat which ran from a weir on the River Yeo by Frankmarsh Woods.

In 2002 a continuous merry-go-round of traffic is found at Mermaid Cross with vehicles converging on this roundabout from the directions of North Walk, Pilton and Braunton. Before Rolle Bridge was built people would have to travel via Pilton to cross the River Yeo.

The Pilton Area

Before following the circular route around the town a road leading northwards takes you along Pilton Causeway to Pilton, which was once, like Newport, separate from the town of Barnstaple. The River Yeo had to be negotiated on foot at low tide before the bridge was built.

Sheepmongers and tanneries were housed along Pilton Causeway and until 1900 parkland bordered both sides of the road. Pilton Park, around which the River Yeo flows, is the same today, but what we know as Yeo Vale was once a marshy area locals called the floating dock. On the 1903 map there are only large houses opposite the park and ten terrace houses along Yeo Vale Road, with another eight along Riddell Avenue. St George's Road and the other interlinking roads are only sketched in.

In the mid 1930s Pilton Bridge was moved when North Road (New Road to us locals) was built through the grounds of Pilton House and Raleigh Park as a bypass for traffic travelling to Ilfracombe via Muddiford and to Lynton via Shirwell.

Another area of Pilton that must have a mention is Raleigh (pronounced Rawleigh). This is tucked away under the hillside of North Road alongside the River Yeo. It is here that Shapland and Petter started their cabinet works in 1864. Before this the area had been the home of the woollen works where Barnstaple Baize was made and transported around the world. Here also was a lace factory and later a laundry. Over the years, too, came Mr Roth's sausage-skin factory, an engineering works and a plastics factory.

Lionel Weston and Owen Knill told me of their childhood memories of Raleigh. Lionel has lived in Raleigh Cottages all his life and Owen's mother had a shop built alongside their home. This was a general store and the main customers were workers from the Raleigh Laundry.

Owen's mother made her own ice-cream. He would have to collect the ice from the Ice Factory in Rolle Street and hurry home where the process of making the ice-cream took place. A powder was put in a central churn, the milk added and the churn continually rotated. As Owen said, child power was cheap in those days so he got the pleasure of this job!

Owen and Lionel recall the happy times they had when they were children and although the people in their 'village' were not well off they always looked after one another. They remember Mr Barrow who lived at 7 Raleigh Cottages, who turned his front rooms into a shop which sold everything, and Mrs Gould who lived at Number 21 and kept pigs in the garden.

Lionel said it was not unusual to go out into their back garden and see the woman in Number 3 talking across the gardens to the woman in Number 20! Neighbours would often share out their vegetables – if one person had too many carrots they would give them away or exchange them for peas or beans. If someone had an old boiler hen they would cook it and then perhaps share it with a neighbour. There were no means of freezing or storing food in those days so it had to be eaten. Lionel's wife Yvonne also recalled that they had a metal wire mesh food safe on the wall in the kitchen to keep off the flies. And the nearest they got to a fridge was a marble slab.

Like Raymond Wickham, who lived in Yeo Vale Road, they all remember the Lynton railway that ran at the bottom of their gardens and the train nicknamed the Lynton Billy.

Long before St George's Road extended to join Derby Road, Raymond, with his brothers and their pals, would follow a path which ran from the St Mary's Road area to Raleigh. It took them over a bridge that crossed the River Yeo by Mr Roth's sausage-skin factory and then another bridge that went over the railway line. People from the Derby and Yeo Vale area would walk along the railway line up through Frankmarsh Wood to picnic and swim in the deep pools by the weir. Raymond would also go 'cladding' for eels, using one of his mother's darning needles with a length of thread and a big juicy worm from the garden.

Boutport Street

We return now to the town and the roundabout at the end of Pilton Causeway. Before the road relief scheme was built the Fire Station was on one corner with Padfield's furniture shop opposite. Next to it was Watts Dairy and legend has it that a tunnel ran under this building from the Castle Mound to the priory at Pilton. It is a fact that when Burgess the builders were renovating the property in the early 1950s they found what could have been an entrance to a tunnel and a sword embedded in the wall.

Raymond Wickham comes up with another suggestion. He believes that if there was a tunnel its destination was more likely to be the priory at Rackfield (an area between Coronation Street and Mill Leat on Pilton Causeway). He points out that to get to Pilton Priory the tunnel would have had to go under the River Yeo and up the hill at Pilton.

Two places of worship were built at this end of the street in the mid 1800s – the Baptist Church which is still going strong, and the Wesleyan Chapel which was demolished some time ago to make way for housing accommodation for the elderly.

The building that is the Conservative Club at the time of writing was erected in the late 1800s as the Assembly Rooms. It was built with public subscription as a social club and dances and balls were held there. It also had rooms for playing billiards and cards.

The Bull Inn stood opposite the entrance to Vicarage Street, which led to the Derby lace factory and the streets of lace-workers' cottages. The house on the corner of Vicarage Street named 'Choweree' was for many years a doctors' surgery. The next street that emerges on to Boutport Street is Joy Street and it is here that the East Gate was sited.

Left: *Lionel Weston as a boy at work at Pitt Farm, Raleigh in 1942. Also in the photograph, left to right: Joan Prizland, Margaret Watts (the little girl), Maureen ? and Bill Turner.*

✌ *Boutport Street* ☙

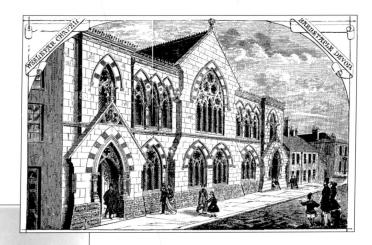

Right: *A lithograph of a wooden carving of the Wesleyan Chapel in Boutport Street. The building was designed by Alexander Lauder.*

Below: *The Bull Inn, Boutport Street opposite Vicarage Street, c.1875. Today this is an entrance to the Green Lane Shopping Centre.*

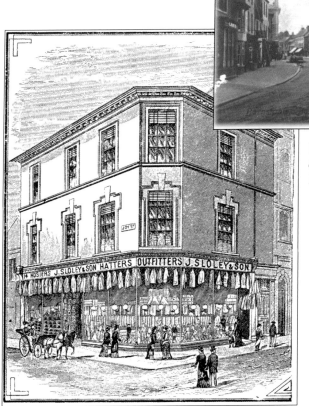

Below: *View of Boutport Street, c.1900. The house on the right with a man outside was demolished and is now the wide road into Queen Street.*

Left: *A lithograph of an etching on zinc plate of J. Sloley & Son Outfitters on the corner of Boutport Street and Joy Street.*

Below: *Boutport Street showing the Fire Station on the right with Padfields opposite.*

Right: *Ken Ayre as a young lad is somewhere in the congregation at this event in 1938 to raise funds to build a new Thorne Memorial Church Sunday School on this ground in Bear Street. He recalls that they were invited to buy a brick for 3d.*

Left: *A coach and horses outside the Royal Mews Stables in Bear Street, c.1910.*

Right: *Herbert Yendell outside his shop in Boutport Street and George Barrow who worked for the firm for many years.*

Women selling from their panniers outside the Corn Market (now Queen's Theatre). The notice on the wall reads 'National Insurance Act, Rechabites', which dates this picture to around 1911.

The Pannier Market.

Queen Anne's Chapel, the grammar school until the early-twentieth century.

Bear Street

Bear Street, named after the de la Barre family who provided several mayors for the town, eventually leads away from the town towards Goodleigh, Bratton Fleming and Exmoor. Number 1 Bear Street was the original shop where Herbert Yendell, a Loxhore farmer's son, started his saddlery business in 1901. He later moved to larger premises almost opposite in Boutport Street where they had stabling. In 1967 his son Morley was commissioned to make a new set of leather work for Exeter Sheriff's coach and horses for the centenary celebrations. Mark Yendell, the third generation, later took over the business, which moved into the High Street.

Further into Bear Street an old inn was demolished to make way for the Thorne Memorial Hall. Ken Ayre recalls as a small boy attending open-air meetings here with his parents. Money-raising events were held where people would buy a brick to help with the cost of the new building.

At the top of Bear Street near the crossroads with Alexandra Road and Gaydon Street stood the Royal Mews Stables. Horses and cabs could be hired here and a coach-and-horse service ran from Newport to the town centre on market days.

Back in Boutport Street, the Queen's Hall was first built in 1855 as the Albert Hall and then, after being rebuilt following a wartime fire, was renamed the Queen's Theatre. The Albert Hall was on the first floor with the Corn Market on the ground floor. The Pannier Market with Butcher's Row beside it was

also built in 1855 and replaced a meat market and slaughterhouses which caused a health hazard and sent obnoxious smells around the centre of the town. Ornate pillars were built at each end of Butcher's Row but with lorries becoming larger and continually causing them damage it was decided to remove them completely. The Pannier Market was so named because farmers' wives would bring their produce in panniers to sell at the Friday market while the farmers were busy at the Cattle Market. Before the Pannier Market was built the women sat in the High Street with their produce.

Travelling down Boutport Street we pass Queen Street, a wide road at the time of writing but until the middle of the twentieth century just a very narrow entrance to what was then called Back Lane. Here was a maze of narrow cobbled streets and during the slum clearances of the 1950s and '60s this part of the town was demolished and redesigned.

Horwood Almshouses, 1930. Mrs Suffolk standing in the doorway on the left was Tom Stribling's grandmother.

Opposite Queen Street is a pedestrian lane called Paternoster Row, which goes through to the High Street, passing Queen Anne's Chapel where in the late 1600s French refugees who had arrived in Barnstaple to escape Protestant persecution were allowed to continue their worship. This building became Barnstaple's first grammar school where John Gay the dramatist was a pupil.

The Parish Church, with its crooked spire, stands beside the chapel with Church Lane crossing between them. Church Lane has eight almshouses, built by merchant Thomas Horwood, and a school erected by his wife Alice Horwood in 1659 for the education of poor girls.

High Street

Let us now walk along the High Street from the far end – the North Gate, which was demolished in 1842.

Leading off on the left is Green Lane. Its cobbled entry probably looks little different from 200 years ago, but now it ends within a few hundred yards at the rear entrance to the Green Lanes shopping centre. What was once a lane with cul-de-sacs of terraced cottages, workshops, stables, dairies, bicycle works and later garages is now a monument to the twentieth-century love of retail shopping. The High Street today has the same multitude of shopping outlets as any other town in the country but you just have to look up to their first-floor façades to really step back into the history of this ancient borough.

The first exit on the right is Gammon Walk where there were once 12 houses closely packed. This lane leads out to Tuly Street and the modern library on the site where Mr Dornat once produced 'delicious and healthful' fruit beverages. One of the town's slaughterhouses also stood in Tuly Street and the Friday Cattle Market was held here until its closure after the Foot and Mouth epidemic in 2001. This meeting-point for farmers from the coast to the moors is no longer viable in a town throttled with traffic – a sad conclusion for a country market town.

Where the National Westminster Bank stands was the site of the Literary and Scientific Institution – later the Art School – founded by William Rock in 1845.

Joy Street is named after Chief Justice Joye, who visited the town in Elizabethan times, and opposite is Holland Walk with small interesting shops on each side of this modern yet medieval-looking lane. (I am told this was not so in days when a butcher had his shop there with a slaughterhouse at the rear!)

On the corner of Butcher's Row stands the Guildhall, which houses many of the town's treasures. The Magistrates Courts were once held here and underneath was the town's first Police Station. The meetings of the Town Council are still held here at the time of writing.

On the Wednesday preceding 20 September every year Barnstaple's fair starts at the Guildhall with speeches of welcome and a toast of spiced ale made to a secret recipe. The white glove of welcome is extended from a top window. The Mayor and Corporation stand on the steps of the Guildhall whilst the Senior Beadle reads the proclamation of the fair opening, which is repeated at both the South and West Gates (or, rather, where they once stood). Further along High Street we come to Cross Street and it was here that the High Cross stood.

Until the Middle Ages the High Street spanned only the areas between Joy Street and Cross Street. The other ends were North Gate Street and South Gate Street. Down to the South Gate were once private houses with huge gardens. Gradually, small shops began trading in this part of the street and where, in 2002, there is a pasty shop was once the Post Office, which later became Raymond's Bakery Shop.

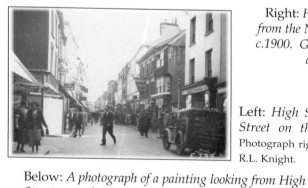

Right: High Street seen from the North Gate end, c.1900. Green Lane leads away to the left.

Left: High Street, with Joy Street on the left, c.1950. Photograph right and below by R.L. Knight.

Below: *A photograph of a painting looking from High Street towards North Gate with Blue Coat School above (the boys on the left could be pupils of the school).*

Below: *The Temperance Hotel in Joy Street, with Thomas' Drapers in foreground and High Street in background, c.1900.*

❧§ *High Street* ❧❧

OLD "BARUM" SERIES

Borough of Barnstaple.

Proclamation for the Fair.

THE MAYOR of this BOROUGH doth hereby give notice that there is a FREE FAIR within this Borough for all manner of persons to BUY and SELL within the same, which fair begins on this day WEDNESDAY, and shall continue until 12 o'clock on the night of FRIDAY, during which time the Mayor chargeth and commandeth on HIS MAJESTY'S behalf all manner of persons repairing to this Town and FAIR DO KEEP the KING'S PEACE

AND that all BUYERS and SELLERS do deal justly and truly and do use true WEIGHTS and MEASURES and that they duly pay their TOLL, STALLAGE and other DUTIES upon pain that shall fall thereon.

AND if any OFFENCES, INJURY or WRONG shall be committed or done by or to any person or persons within this TOWN FAIR and LIBERTY the same shall be redressed according to JUSTICE and the LAWS of this REALM.

God Save the King.

Right: Awaiting the Fair proclamation at the Guildhall in Butcher's Row, c.1920.

OLD GUILDHALL

Above: Sketch drawn by Jonathan Lomas of the Guildhall in High Street opposite Cross Street and spanning the entrance to the Parish Church. The building, designed in the style of Exeter's Guildhall, was purchased in 1532 by the Town Council but was demolished in 1826 when the present-day Guildhall was opened.

Above: Proclamation ceremony in the Guildhall, 1930.
Photograph R.L. Knight.

Right: Civic group in Fair proclamation procession along the Strand in 1979. Senior Town Beadle Graham White (front left), Mayor W.H. Luxton (centre) and Town Beadle Chris Hammett (right).

Above: *The High Street in the late 1920s.*
Photograph R.L. Knight.

Right: *South Gate end of the High Street,
c.1965.*

Top right: *Entrance to Brannam's Pottery in
Litchdon Street.*

The *North Devon Herald* and *North Devon Journal* were both at this end of the street until they merged in 1941 and went into the offices at Number 96 where the newspaper still is today.

It may be remembered by some people that beside Cummings Umbrella Shop (Dayman's Outfitters in 2002) was an alleyway that led to Pengelly's Court (or Hearson's Place). Abby Drew told me that his grandmother lived here. There were seven houses, one fig tree and a water pump. Raymond Wickham remembers Mrs Earle who played the violin on the corner of Butcher's Row and also lived in Pengelly's Court. The houses were used as accommodation during the war for evacuees but soon after were condemned and demolished.

Back at the South Gate near the Square stands the Royal and Fortescue Hotel, an impressive building dating back to around 1780. The building next door was once the Golden Lion Hotel, which was probably the headquarters of the merchant adventures in the mid 1600s.

From here stagecoaches left daily at 7.30a.m. (except Sundays) for Tiverton, Taunton, Salisbury and London. On three days a week coaches departed for Plymouth. In 1831 a rival service started from the Fortescue, bound for London via Crediton and Exeter, leaving at 11.30a.m. and arriving the next day at 4.00p.m.

The Golden Lion was converted into a bank in 1936 and great care was taken to preserve the plaster-moulded ceilings, which date back to 1629. These can still be enjoyed as the building is now a restaurant.

The Square, with seven roads entering and leaving it around the central floral roundabout, has seen many parades over the centuries, from military to carnival, and celebrations from coronations to the cessation of wars and the welcoming of a new year. The Albert Clock silently oversees all proceedings.

To complete our historical tour of the town we leave the Square by Litchdon Street, once the main London Road. It was here that Charles Brannam established his pottery in 1879 and the wealthy merchant, John Penrose, built almshouses in 1627. Across from the far end of the street stood the North Devon Infirmary, built in 1826 by public subscription. At the time of writing a residential complex, in keeping with the style of the old hospital, stands in its place. This brings us back to Taw Vale and Rock Park.

Chapter Three
LIFE ON & AROUND
THE RIVER TAW

View of the River Taw with Long Bridge in the distance, as seen from Rock Park.

The River Taw rises on the barren heights of Dartmoor and cascades over rocky moorland until it reaches the peacefulness of the Taw Valley. In summer it quietly meanders along its winding course through meadows and woods, but in winter this can all change within a few hours after heavy rain. The river then becomes a swollen torrent and often the banks are breached, making the meadow valleys a sea of water. Flooding has long been a problem for the town planners of Barnstaple as when the tide arrives at the town and meets the Taw the only place for the excess water to go is over the river banks and into the parks and streets. After some clever civil engineering the problem has been alleviated, but many people have memories of the regular flooding of both Pilton and Rock Parks, and especially Taw Vale.

Sheila Edwards, who lived in Gloster Road, recalls one occasion during the Second World War when she was walking to a dance in the town. When she got to Victoria Road she found it flooded and, with no way round the water, she says, she hoisted up her best dance dress, took off her shoes and waded through. She arrived at the dance a trifle bedraggled but she wasn't going to let a little flood water spoil her night out!

Although there is little documentation of shipbuilding in the town before the late 1700s it is known that this was an important industry in the town. There were four boatyards in and around Barnstaple; one at Pottington, one at Rolle Quay and another at Pilton Quay. On the River Taw the yard belonging to John Wilkey was opposite the entrance to Litchdon Street, behind what is now Riversdale (remembering that Taw Vale was then gardens which ran down to the river). Robert Westacott bought this yard and for the next four generations the Westacott family was associated with Barnstaple shipbuilding, until it ceased in the early 1900s.

The demand for larger ships in the mid 1850s led to difficulties for the yard as larger boats could not pass through the arches of the bridge. The then owner, John Westacott (Robert's son), decided to relocate to the other side of the bridge at Bridge Wharf (later Shapland and Petter), allowing them to continue trading after the other shipbuilders had closed down.

Percy Westacott, great-great-grandson of John, returned to the town at the beginning of the First World War when he was given the task by the Government to build reinforced concrete ships. Barnstaple was chosen not only because of the Westacott link with the town but also due to its obviously ideal situation, on a river estuary, close to the sea, with a good railway link and huge deposits of gravel, which was needed for the cement. Also there was no problem with obtaining a workforce. Men travelled from the depressed areas of the country to join the project. Two such were Bill Owen and Fred Nicholls, who came from Swansea to find

Aerial view over the River Taw showing slipways for concrete ships built during the First World War.
Photograph R.L. Knight.

work. They lodged with the Goodings family in Clifton Street and later married the two daughters, Gwen and Dora. When the shipyard closed they went back to Wales, but Fred and Dora later returned to Barnstaple and were the licensees of the Great Western Hotel in Trinity Street.

It was not only men that worked at the shipyard; as Raymond Wickham told me his mother Lottie was employed there during the war. Her job was to bend the reinforcing bars which shaped the concrete ships. She had explained to him that the foreman would draw a pattern on the ground with chalk and the women had to bend the metal to fit it.

The shipyard was built on the marshland between the railway line and the river at the beginning of Anchor Wood, next to what had been Westacott's yard. It made seven concrete ships. They were easily built and no engines were fitted as they were to be towed across the Atlantic in convoy, but not all

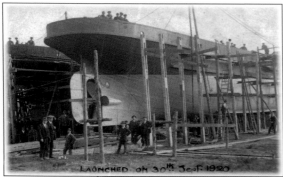

Above: *A concrete ship during construction. It was launched 30 September 1920.*

Taken from a view above Bridge Buildings, a concrete ship is seen after launching. On the back of the postcard is written: **3rd F/c Ship to be launched at Barnstaple. Launched 29.9.18 at 7 o'clock. Smashed up on or about 9.12.18 through carelessness.**

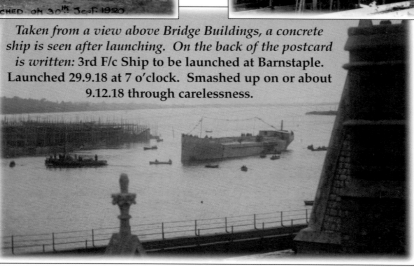

Above: *Two concrete ships with workmen on board before being launched.*

This picture shows the concrete ship after it had been launched and had crashed into the Quay wall. Cecil Bale, who worked at Shapland and Petters, witnessed the event and took this photograph. He wrote on the back, 'I was in the drawing and design office'.

successfully! One was beached at Instow and another broke its back as it left the slipway. Cecil Bale, who at the time was an apprentice draughtsman with Shapland and Petter, was sitting in the drawing room at the factory and captured the event on his camera. Frank Bromley also recalls this occasion and remembers watching the ship as it was launched and then drifted across the river until it hit the wall by the bus station.

By 1922 shipbuilding had ceased in Barnstaple but the cement-making business continued and this, of course, called for a continuous supply of sand and gravel. Supplies came from sandbanks in the estuary from as near to Bideford Bar as the barges could get at low tide. Bideford Bar is a dangerous sandbank that only substantial vessels can negotiate and over which the Atlantic breakers crash.

The sandbanks have interesting names such as Zulu Point, Crow Point, Spratt Ridge, Klondyke, Paiges Flats, Sewage Pit (where rough gravel was mainly found) and Konica, which was close to where Fremington Pottery had been and where the bargemen found an abundance of discarded clay pipes with bulls and fishes' heads on.

I have spent hours talking to two men who worked the barges for most of their lives. Patrick Moore and John Drayton first met at Trinity Street School and are still close friends and, at the time of writing, also close neighbours. John's father, William Drayton (known as 'Fairy'), came to Barnstaple from Bournemouth with his friend 'Darky' Legg to build the concrete ships. William married Rose Popham from Higher Church Street and John was one of their nine children. After the shipyard closed William worked at Rolle Quay

unloading the boats of timber, slag and flour. John's first job was as a furniture remover – a trade he returned to after his life on the barges.

Patrick Moore comes from a long line of river men. His grandfather was William Moore, who was better known as Billie Moore of the Boat Station. The family lived at Hardaway Head (now the multi-storey car park). Patrick's first job in 1948 was with his father George, a bargee on the *Rowena*, which belonged to Rawle, Gammon and Baker whose premises were on the River Yeo by Rolle Bridge. Patrick remembers being paid £1 a day for loading 15 tons of gravel on and off the barge. This was carried out with the help of a crane, but in his father's time they had to shovel it into the barge from the gravel pits and, when they arrived back at the quay again, unload it by hand into the waiting lorries. Before these times it would have been loaded onto a horse and cart.

Working hours were stipulated by the tide times and this meant the men started as early as 2a.m. and as late as 11a.m. There was great skill in manoeuvring these boats onto and off the sandbanks. The barge came to rest on the chosen bank as the tide went out and the men then had a limited amount of time to load the sand before the tide came back and lifted them off again. The nearer to Bideford Bar they moored, the less time they had to complete the loading. It was on such an occasion on Zulu Bank that Patrick experienced a tragic accident. On 27 February 1959 three barges went out to load gravel. Patrick's uncle, Bill Moore, was the skipper of the *Nellie Ann* with Jimmy Patience as the mate. The *ACM's* crew included Jimmy Passmore and Freddie Hill. Patrick was skipper of the *Nellie* and Roy Scott was his mate.

The Moores

Left: *Jack Avery, the great-grandfather of Patrick Moore. Jack lived in Wells Street, and worked as a fisherman on the Taw and as a stevedore.*

Right: *Billy Moore at his Boat Station by Rock Park.*

Inset: *Patrick Moore on board the barge RH13 in 1961.*

The Moore family enjoying a picnic after filling up the barge with sand and gravel.

John Drayton and Patrick Moore are pictured loading gravel onto the **Advance (on left)**.
The barge **P.K.H.** *is pictured on the right.*

Patrick told me that there was a rough sea on the way out to Zulu Point. 'Heavy swell with large breakers', he recalls. He hadn't been out to this bank before, so his uncle showed him how to moor the boat. Pat had a couple of attempts to ground the *Nellie* and when he did he touched down further out than the other two barges, which meant less time to load up before the tide came in. Pat refloated without any trouble and waited for the other two barges. The sea got rougher and the other two barges kept bumping together. The jarring knocked the oakum filling out of the *Nellie Ann's* seams and when the waves came over the boat the water entered between the wooden planks, making her unstable. Patrick watched helplessly as his uncle and Jimmy Patience clung to the funnel before being washed overboard. Both men were drowned despite the other crews' attempts to save them. Jimmy was found at low tide at Crow Rocks but it was six weeks before the river eventually gave up Bill Moore.

On a less sombre note Patrick told me of other misadventures in his bargee's life. The first sinking of the *Nellie* was only a few yards from Rolle Quay. The entrance to the River Yeo from the estuary is a very precarious one that needs a great deal of skill to negotiate. There are two large upright poles in the riverbed which are known as the 'dolphins'. You had to turn the boat against the tide, which was running at 6–7 knots, and aim at the narrow entrance of the river to get between the dolphins. On this particular night Patrick was working with John Drayton and they were entering the dolphins. Pat, who was at the helm, hit the railway bridge which spans the river. They carried on up the river but by the time they got to Stanbury's Flour Mill the boat had filled with water. They both chuckle at the memory that there was only time for John to dash down below to save Patrick's gold watch and chain before they abandoned ship. To those of us who have seen these barges chug up the river so heavily laden with sand that the water washes over the deck and the crew are up to their ankles in water, it is no surprise that they can sink so fast.

The *Nellie's* second and final sinking happened on a night when she was working with another barge, the *Speck*, at Crow Point. Again, Patrick and John were on board. They explained that it was common practice when working at Crow for the first barge off the bottom to assist the other to get afloat by throwing a rope to tow them off. The crew of the *Speck* threw a rope to the *Nellie* but this broke. The second attempt was also disastrous as the fresh rope got entangled in *Nellie's* propellers. Both barges and crews ended up beached at Crow Point and the only way home was in a small dinghy with only one oar to paddle their way up the river. The *Speck* was later refloated but the *Nellie* had broken her back and remained on the beach for many years before she disintegrated.

The *RH13* replaced the *Nellie*. This new barge belonged to Bob Harris of Harris & Son the builders.

Barges

Above: *Crow Point in 1957. George Moore is on board the barge* Nellie *in the foreground. The other bargees are George Huxtable and Paul Michael.*

Below: *The RH13 coming alongside Castle Quay in 1960.*

Eddie Jewell is on the left, with Tom Stribling on the right, loading sand onto their barge with the help of a young lad.

The winter of 1963 when the RH13 had to be towed home through the ice-packed Taw.

Pat remembers that in 1963 the River Taw froze over as they were nearing home at Castle Quay and they had to be towed through the ice for the last few yards of the journey. After a couple of days laid up, Pat decided to take the barge back to work but they did not get far as they hit an 'iceberg' near Pottington and broke the propeller.

Patrick worked on the barges until the late 1960s when less sand and gravel were being excavated from the estuary. Of the 25 barges in the Taw and Torridge in the 1940s only seven were still in operation by this time.

Another river man was Thomas Ernest Stribling, born in 1922 in Princess Street, Derby, the son of Ernest and Rose. Tom left the Blue Coat School at the age of 14 and wanted to join the Merchant Navy but his father wouldn't allow it, so young Tommy went to work at Ham's Furniture Shop in the High Street where he did his apprenticeship as an upholsterer. He says he hated it and finally joined the Merchant Navy in 1941, where he stayed for 11 years. On his return home he married Mary Lock and spent the next ten years working on the RGB sand barges. For the first four years he was on his own with a small 15-ton barge. He would take the boat up to Crow Point on the ebb tide, fill it by hand and return on the high tide. Later, there were two men and a larger barge and depending on where they moored they had between two to four hours to load before the sea came in again.

In 1960 when Tom's uncle, Bill Stribling, retired as river pilot, Tom took on the job. He did not have any written qualifications, only experience and knowledge of the shifting sands on the River Taw estuary. He put out buoys to mark the safe route for the big vessels that came up the river, such as the *Stan Woolaway*, *William Woolaway* and *Ron Woolaway*. There was also the *Arkle Taw* and *Arkle Tamar*, which carried rough gravel from Lynmouth and fine sand from Wales. Their cargoes came to Castle Quay to be conveyed to Woolaways builders yard at Sticklepath. The marker buoys had to be put out once a fortnight, as the sand is so fine that it shifts quickly with the tides. Tommy says that in summertime the river silts up more quickly than in winter, when the heavy rain that comes down the river washes out the riverbed naturally.

To pilot the boats up the river Tom would drive to Fremington Quay, row a dingy out to the boat and bring it into Rolle Quay. The larger boats could only get into Rolle Quay six or seven times a fortnight on the higher tides and then they only had a 12-hour turnaround time. Unlike with the small barges, the railway swingbridge had to be opened to allow the larger barges passage into the quay. When tides and train timetables clashed this meant holding up the trains, so the railway paid Tom a fee to inform them when the ships were due.

Frank Kidwell was a signalman on the swing-bridge and watched Tom at work. He told me how much respect he had for Tom. 'It took an awful lot of nerve to get those big boats through the dolphins,' said Frank.

Tom's other occupation, between 1950 and 1987, was as a licensed salmon fisherman. He told me that sometimes his piloting work would only take up three hours of the day, so he would then spend the rest of the day fishing.

Fishing the River Taw has been not only a hobby but also a way of life for centuries. Most of the stories told to me come from men who as young boys lived near the river, which served as their playground.

The Rivers Taw and Yeo were not only places of work but also where the people spent their recreation time. There are few who do not remember or have not heard of the Boat Station. This was a large wooden hut moored on the Taw by Rock Park and from here you could hire a dinghy to row up or down the river. Most people refer to it as Billy Moore's Boat Station. It was owned by the Council and in 1921 William Gee leased it from them. William was from London, where he had met Clara who was working in the London house of the vicar of Pilton. At the onset of the First World War William joined the Army and the family returned to live at Pilton Quay. William's health was seriously damaged when he was gassed in France and so Clara, with six young children, had to be the main breadwinner. It was then that the family moved to 4 Litchdon Street where Clara opened a fruit and vegetable shop. William hired out the boats from the Boat Station and Billy Moore rented the back of the boat-house where he repaired bicycles. Between them the two men dredged the river twice a year from New Bridge to Long Bridge, working from their small boats either side of the river. William also taught swimming in the river. There is an advert, which reads:

View of the Taw from Seven Brethren Bank with Billy Moore's Boat Station moored by the entrance to Rock Park, c.1930. The North Devon Infirmary and Trinity Church can be seen in the background.

The Taw salmon fishermen in the 1950s. Left to right, back row: Arthur Nightingale, Joe Parminter-Manning, Reg Irwin (Pompi), Ned Hill, Bill Wakely; front row: Bill Nightingale (son of Arthur), Jimmy Passmore, Bill Passmore, Tom Stribling, Bert Bowden. In 1950 there were 32 licensed boats with four men to a boat. In 1987 there were only 16 boats left with two men in each boat.

Facilities for Bathing at Barnstaple.
Bathing Hut for undressing   *Only 4d*
Hire of Costume   *2d*
Hire of Towel   *2d*
School Children Undressing   *Only 2d*
Private Swimming Lessons – Moderate Charges.
Apply W. GEE of the Boat House, Rock Park.

Mr Heppenstall, the headmaster of Ashleigh Road School, used to take the boys down to the river and with the help of William Gee taught them to swim. William also taught them to dive from a board on the opposite side of the bank.

Billy Moore succeeded William Gee at the boat-house. There are many tales of this boatman and all are memories of affection. Billy was crippled with arthritis and the boys would go up the river to collect his boats which had been left on the bank. Billy paid half a crown for their retrieval. One 'boy' admitted to me that he and his mates encouraged people to leave boats upriver so they could earn their pocket money. They could also earn a penny or two by rowing the boats for off-duty nurses up to Bishops Tawton, where they would all have a picnic and wait for the next tide to take them back.

William and Clara on their wedding day in 1910.

Billy Moore had his workshops in Belle Meadow and John Shaddick remembers that the boys used to hang around watching Billy repairing the boats. John told me that in 1928 Billy lost one of his boats and in 1952 divers were inspecting the foundations of the iron railway bridge and under Long Bridge there they found it! John told me that it wasn't long before Billy had the engine going again. The boat itself was not much use so Billy gave it to two lads who helped him around the boat-house. They later had a disagreement over its ownership so one of them cut it in half!

John Shaddick also worked on the sand barges for a few years with his brothers Dennis and Len. They spent most of their young lives in and around the river. John says that one of his earliest memories is of his father rowing them down to Yelland to collect mussels. His brother Len says they used to spend most of their free time playing on the river, especially around the boat-house at Rock Park. They would make mud slides on the bank and Len recalls that their swimming costumes were old jumpers with the necks sewn up. They put their legs through the armholes and secured the waist with a piece of binder twine. He said that when they went

Right: *A boating trip on the Taw, c.1920.*

Left: *William Gee and Mr Heppenstall teaching the boys of Ashleigh Road School to swim in the River Taw, 1921.*

Left: *Billy Moore in his boat,* The Polly, *by the iron railway bridge over the Taw, c.1930.*

into the water the weight of the wet wool would pull the 'costume' down to their knees. Anything that floated constituted a boat. They used old oil drums, planks of wood and lengths of rope. Len loved to go fishing for flatfish in the pools under Long Bridge and says he quite often caught 'monsters'!

Len later had his own boat called *Hilda* on the riverbank. He told me the story of how one morning Ernie Kelly, who was a street cleaner, called at their house in Belle Meadow and said to Len's father, 'Tell your boy that when he goes poaching to cover up the fish'. When Len later inspected his boat there, sure enough there was a large salmon in the bow wrapped in a towel where Ernie had seen it. Len carried home the fish and showed his father, who was pleased with the 12lb specimen. When I asked Len how the fish got in the boat he told me that it must have jumped in from the river. I wonder if the water bailiff would have believed him!

Flounder fishing has long been popular on the Taw and at the beginning of the twenty-first century it has seen a resurgence. It was reported in an angling magazine that Stuart Webber and Julian Stainer had caught over 1,000 flounder in the past season. This included a prize-winning 2lb 14oz fish, caught by Stuart.

John Shaddick and his wife Pat still have a passion for life on the water and spend all of their spare time on their boat, which is kept at Rolle Quay. In retirement John has also taken up painting and poetry and often depicts his memories of the river and the area around Rock Park.

Right: *Dennis Shaddick, who loved messing about on the river and later worked on the barges.*

Below: *Brothers John, Dennis and Ivor Shaddick with Terry Hill on Seven Brethren Bank with one of their maritime creations.*

Right: *John Shaddick in retirement with his painting of Billy Moore's Boat Station.*

Childhood Memories

An avenue of elm trees stood so proud
The tops seemed to touch the clouds.
They stood on the banks of the River Taw
Walking through them made me feel so small.

I remember standing with a frown
The day they cut those elm trees down.
Along Taw Vale and over the bridge
There were fairy light flowers
Set in wrought-iron grids.
Colours reflected in the river at night
Oh it was such a wonderful sight!

Billy Moore's boat-house that's gone too
When I was a lad I was the crew.
The boat-house was a place for people to go,
To hire a boat and go for a row.

Alas they are just memories now and I feel I must
Record them for posterity with my paints and brush.

John Shaddick
May 2001

Chapter Four

RIVER YEO & ROLLE QUAY

This bridge over the River Yeo was built in 1829. Before it was built people had to travel via Pilton to get to the Pottington area. The bridge could swing open to allow the passage of large boats between Rolle Quay and the timber yards of Rawle, Gammon & Baker and Pilton Quay.

The River Yeo is a series of tributaries which rise on the heights of Exmoor. Gathering in size and speed they meet below Chelfham and enter the town between Raleigh and Yeo Vale, flowing under Pilton Bridge to the once busy port of Pilton Quay. The river becomes tidal here and meanders around Pilton Park before turning to travel along Rolle Quay to join the River Taw.

A swingbridge was built across the river in 1829, connecting the North Gate end of the town to Rolle Quay. Until this time, people travelling to Pottington, Braunton and anywhere west of the town had to go around Pilton. The bridge was later replaced by another swingbridge and in 1978 major traffic disruption was caused when the present-day fixed road bridge was built.

At the time of writing, Rolle Quay has a wall alongside the river and is lined with homes and commercial buildings. A century ago this was a bustling port which saw boats delivering coal, slag, grain, agricultural goods and animal feed. A railway along the quayside enabled the easy loading and unloading of boats.

Arthur Squires, who for many years worked for John How & Company, gave me an insight into his working life. The firm sold coal, corn, agricultural goods and animal-feed products and was situated next to the Rolle Quay public house. In 1939 the 15-year-old

The River Yeo, as it meanders around Pilton Park.

✥ *Rolle Quay* ✥

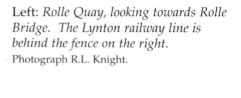

Left: *Rolle Quay, looking towards Rolle Bridge. The Lynton railway line is behind the fence on the right.*
Photograph R.L. Knight.

Right: *The* Sally Ann *alongside Victoria Flour Mills, Rolle Quay, c.1930.*

Above: *Rolle Quay with Brunswick Wharf on the right, c.1890. What is the man in the right foreground doing in the water?*

Arthur saw a job advertised at John How's. His mother went with him to the interview, but only after his father had attended another interview was Arthur taken on for the princely sum of 6s.0d. a week, with a 2s.6d. rise yearly for five years. Arthur gave his mother 2s.6d. a week for his keep and after a weekly payment of 2s.6d. for his bicycle was left with 1s. for himself. After six months Arthur rebelled! Every quarter day the firm's bills had to be sent out to customers and he had to write them all by hand. This meant staying at work until 9p.m. with no extra payment. After a while Arthur asked Mr Glover, the branch manager, if the firm was going to give him a rise for this overtime. He remembers that Mr Glover looked over his horn-rimmed glasses and said, 'Whatever are you saying, Arthur?' However, after due deliberation Arthur's weekly pay went up to 7s.6d. and by the age of 17 he was earning 12s.6d.

Workmen outside John How & Company, with Cecil Wotton pictured in the centre.

Not long after this Arthur was advised to attend a meeting at the Mermaid Hotel (later the North Gate Hotel). To his surprise he found he was at a Union meeting, which in those times was a controversial and political 'hot potato'. Men could lose their jobs for either being in a union, or equally, for not belonging to one. Arthur recalls that two overweight men from Bristol were there smoking big cigars and extolling the virtues of the Union movement, and by the end of the evening he found he was a fully-paid member of the National Union of Farm Workers. This obviously benefited Arthur as from the following Friday he was paid 27s.6d. a week.

Arthur told me that Southern Railway shunted trucks of coal and cattle feed at 10.30a.m. and 4.30p.m. daily for loading and discharging. He remembered Walter Stribling, who started work at 9.30a.m. with a donkey-cart and wheel-barrow and continued without a break until 12.30p.m., shovelling coal from the trucks into the wheelbarrow then across the road into John How's cellars. Walter moved 10 to 12 tons in one session. He would then go home for lunch, return in the afternoon and do it all over again. His take-home pay was 10s.6d. a week.

Another well-known name on the quay was coal merchants W. Dalling & Sons. They had an overhead gantry with a bucket that lowered into a railway truck, where a man filled it with the coal. The

A fully-laden sand barge entering the River Yeo through the 'dolphins' at high tide.

Below: *Unloading a ship with the overhead gantry at W. Dalling & Sons on Rolle Quay, c.1930.*
Photograph R.L. Knight.

Below left: *A sand barge coming home under Rolle Bridge with water washing over the deck.*

Left: *Stanbury's Victoria Flour Mills, c.1910. The man with the bowler-hat is the owner, Richard John Stanbury, and the man in the middle is his son Walter. The foreman of the mill, William Henry Locke, is pictured on the right.*

Right: *Frank Kidwell at work, 1962.*

bucket was mechanically raised and swung across to the building for emptying. Arthur also remembers the animal-feed merchants Carder and Perryman. Eric Bolt was their salesman and Tommy Jewell was the lorry driver. Then there were hauliers H.A. Scott with their smart Guy motor lorries, which carried out most of the work for the merchants along the quay. At the far end of the quay and nearest to the mouth of the river stood the large red-brick building of Victoria Flour Mills. Most of their trade came by sea and amongst their boats were the *Bessie Gould*, the *Bessie Clarke*, the *Enid*, the *Edna*, the *B.T.H.*, the *Clara May* and the *Kathleen and May*, which has recently been restored at Bideford. Arthur recalls Captain Clarke of Braunton and Captain Slade of Appledore, as well as the pilot, William Stribling, who would row a dinghy out to the Bideford Bar, board the boats and guide them safely back to Rolle Quay.

Cecil Gammon told me that his father Ernie (known as Dappy) Gammon worked for Stanbury's as a lorry driver and he would deliver flour from Lynton to Okehampton and down into Cornwall. Further information about Victoria Flour Mills came from Elizabeth Isaac, the great-granddaughter of Richard Stanbury who had the mill built in 1898. He had owned water-driven flour-mills at Knowle and Heddon Mill but saw the potential of operating alongside the waterfront and cutting out the cost of transporting the flour by road. When Richard died his son Walter did not want to continue in the business and it was sold to J. Arthur Rank.

Frank Kidwell also has memories of working on Rolle Quay. A railwayman based at the Town Station,

he was responsible for opening the swingbridge to allow large boats through to the quay. Frank told me that river traffic had priority over the trains up to 20 minutes before the top of the tide as this allowed time to refloat any grounded vessels. Frank says it took three men to open and close the bridge and their record was 12 minutes. However, this speed trial did on occasion lead to some mishaps, such as the time when a signalman of rather large proportions could not keep up with the other two men as they operated the capstan. He lost his footing and ended up wedged between the bars of the bridge. On another occasion, during the night, a railwayman was sent from the Junction Station to help and, not being familiar with the job, ended up taking a long walk off a short bridge! The first the others knew was a large splash as the unfortunate man landed in the river.

Frank was also responsible for clearing all the carriages away from the main railway lines and into the sidings along Rolle Quay to allow evening trains from Barnstaple to Ilfracombe and Ilfracombe to Exeter to pass Pottington with a clear track. He said the sidings could take 98 wagons but one evening they had 100 wagons to push along the quay. Frank got the driver to shunt up hard and eventually, with all the buffers compressed, the train cleared the main line. It wasn't long before someone came to tell them that the road near Rolle Bridge was blocked as the wagons had jumped the stop blocks at the end of the line and were now right across the road.

Wet feet were another problem for Frank when working at Rolle Quay. During the spring tides when he was shunting in the sidings the water would often

❧ Rolle Quay Fun ❧

A pub outing outside the Rolle Quay Inn, 1950.

Playmates gathered at Rolle Quay in 1957. At the back is Bobby Hill. Left to right,
back row: Peter Mullins, Janet Draper, Barbara Richardson, ?, ? Rigler;
front row: Barry Draper, ? Rigler, Aiden Morrish, Jimmy Richardson.

be over the axle box on his engine and he would be up to his knees in water. And it was not unknown for him to have to wade out into the River Taw to recover wagon tarpaulins which had floated away on the tide.

Two men who have memories of their boyhood years in and around Rolle Quay are Derek Seymour and Raymond Wickham, whose families lived in Mill Road. Derek, who now lives in Inverkeithing, Fife, told me that his father Bob Seymour worked on the *Rowena* sand barge and was also one of the salmon fishermen. He recalls that the salmon nets were usually spread out on the grass near his home to dry or be repaired. The fishing boat had four oarsmen and a coxswain and apart from nets the men used prangs to spear the flatfish. Night-lines with 50–100 baited hooks were also pegged into the sand or mud at low tide. At the next low tide the men collected the fish and baited up the hooks for the next tide. Derek said that his father sold his fish to Harry Guard in Butcher's Row, except for the few that changed hands in the Rolle Quay Inn.

Raymond, who was born at 19 Mill Road, remembers the day-trippers who came to visit Baron's Pottery at the end of the road. He says he learnt from a very young age that by sitting on his trike on the pavement and smiling sweetly he was rewarded by these visitors with apples, oranges, sweets or chocolate, in particular Five Boys chocolate bars.

In the 1930s Mill Road had little or no traffic so it was quite safe for the children to play in the street, but on one occasion the milkman's dray horse was in the wrong place at the wrong time for Raymond's elder brother Leslie. Coming down the slipway from Rolle Quay to Mill Road on his trolley he could not stop to avoid the horse so went between the horse's fore and hind legs and out the other side without the horse or milkman noticing! Raymond's eldest brother Gordon was a born leader and one day he led his band of 'men' to borrow a 12ft clinker-built fishing boat and 'put to sea' to foreign lands such as Anchor Woods or Pottington. In the afternoon when it was getting dark and storm clouds were gathering the parents began to look for their offspring. They searched in the coal trucks and all the usual hide-outs around the quayside until they heard the cry 'In, out, in, out' and between the dolphins came Gordon at the helm, encouraging his men to row faster through the pouring rain. Gordon later spent the war years at sea in the Indian Ocean and the Mediterranean.

We end this chapter with the childhood memories of Pat Shaddick, née Moles, who was evacuated with her two brothers from Plaistow, London, to live at 4 O'Linda Place, Rolle Quay. This was a row of cottages down steps behind a wall by the steep slipway mentioned above. These cottages were liable to flooding and were demolished after 1958. Pat remembers playing with her friends along Rolle Quay, watching the trucks on the railway line loading and unloading from the boats. The children did not have many toys but they made their own fun playing in the sand left on the quayside and in summer they often went swimming in the River Yeo.

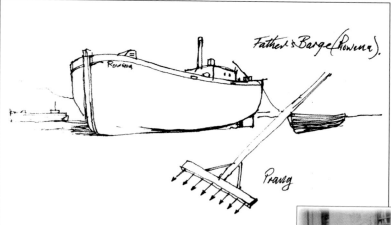

Left: 'Prangs' resembled a garden fork with sharp teeth.
Sketch by Derek Seymour.

Right: *Barbara Richardson outside her home in O'Linda Place, 1955.*

Chapter Five

GONE BUT NOT FORGOTTEN

The Soup Kitchen in the Corn Market, c.1920. The second man on the left is Charles Lake,
who owned the drapery in Boutport Street. Photograph R.L. Knight.

Many streets and areas of Barnstaple conjure up memories for the people who lived and worked in them, including Derby, Azes Lane, Hardaway Head, Queen Street, Trinity Street, Belle Meadow, Zions Place and Silver Street. Many were cleared in the 1950s and the inhabitants rehoused in purpose-built estates on what were then the outskirts of the town. This wholesale demolition is often referred to as 'Barnstaple's slum clearance' and not wanting to be insensitive when talking to people who grew up in these old areas I never refer to them as such. However, it was always made clear to me that although poor they were rich in community spirit and pride. One man told me, 'We had nothing but we had everything.'

In the early 1900s Barnstaple, like most other parts of the country, suffered from poverty, poor housing and water supply, inadequate medical services and harsh working conditions. Today we have Social Services to help the underprivileged but

100 years ago this fell to the gentry, employers and other benefactors. In 1907 Mayor A.J. Reavell and his wife gave a series of five free dinners to the 'poor and old people' of the town. The first was a Boxing Day breakfast for children. Over 800 tickets were applied for but the Albert Hall (now Queen's Theatre) could only hold 500 and another 100 were seated in the Corn Market. A newspaper reported that:

Considering the fact that guests were drawn from the poorest homes in the town, the cleanness and happy appearance of the children were remarkable.

The menu consisted of pea soup, which was prepared in the Soup Kitchen. Meaty pasty (composed of beef and kidney with a layer of potatoes) was supplied by Messrs Rainbow and Carder of Joy Street, and plum pudding was given by Mrs Brooks' café. Carols were sung between each course, then the children formed two queues and filed past the Mayor and Mayoress to collect Christmas gifts. The newspaper said it was 'one of the most delightful treats ever given in Barnstaple.'

The second dinner was arranged by the Committee of the Soup Kitchen and consisted of Irish stew and 'dough boys'. The third feast was for 320 elderly and those who could not attend due to ill health had their dinners sent out to them. The fourth dinner fed 350 children and at the final dinner, Irish stew was served to 750 people.

Newspaper reports of this era are written in great detail and throw light on the level of poverty in the town and also on the part played by the more affluent members of the community. All the local dignitaries and tradesmen who gave their time or goods for these dinners were named in the paper.

The Soup Kitchen mentioned above continued for many years and several people I spoke to remember going to the Albert Hall to collect a jug of pea and ham soup to take home for the family. All say how good this soup was but some felt that there was a stigma attached to receiving it. Derek Seymour, who lived in Mill Road, said his mother insisted he went to the Albert Hall via Green Lane so he was not seen carrying his jug of pea and ham soup in the High Street. 'And it had to be disguised with a towel over the top', he told me, 'but I loved the stuff.'

Raymond Wickham said he used to go with his brother Les on a Saturday to collect the soup, which he remembers as thick and creamy and came with a large hunk of new bread, well worth the 3d. it cost. He said it was their equivalent to today's Little Chef or McDonalds!

People such as GP Dr Richard Harper worked tirelessly to improve the conditions in which so many families lived. What he saw on his rounds spurred him into action. After a visit to one patient in 1943, for instance, he wrote in his diary:

Ten persons in a tiny, sunless, bug and beetle infected house, who were trying to make a good show, but failing because the odds were too great.

Dr Harper arranged for several influential people to visit the houses with him and from this meeting the Barnstaple Slums and Housing Conditions Committee was born. Its Interim Report contained many photographs taken by Dr Harper when he visited patients in these slum areas. It led to the Town Council undertaking a Slum Clearance Programme, which was started in 1954. Around 700 houses were demolished in five years and many of

these were in the Derby area. Derby (pronounced, as it is spelt) was so named as it was built around the lace factory, which had originated from the Midlands town of Derby (pronounced Darby). The houses, many built of cob, were in tightly-packed streets – Union Street, Reform Street, Princess Street, Corsor Street, Higher and Lower Maudlin Streets, Newington Street and parts of Gaydon Street and Richmond Street – and it is from these areas that the rich and colourful memories of men and women who lived there as children have been gathered.

Ernie Ovey was born in Corsor Street in 1929. His parents, Frederick and Jessie, had 15 children of which Ernie remembers seven brothers and four sisters. His grandfather John, who lived in Princess Street, worked at the lace factory until he was 76 years old. Ernie has many memories of his early home, which was a two-up, two-down cottage. The front door led straight into the main living-room, which included a cooking range. At the back of this room was a scullery from whence the stairs went up to the two bedrooms. The children slept three at the top end of a bed and three at the bottom, boys in one bed and girls in another. The baby slept between the parents. Under the stairs was a cupboard where the coal was kept (the coal 'ole). At the back of the house was a small yard and outside toilet. Over the back wall was St Mary Magdalene Church. The choir vestry door was near the wall and Ernie says that on Sundays his timing was perfect as he could jump straight out of bed, dress, leap over the wall and be in his place in the choir in minutes.

Like many children of those times Ernie had a job before and after school hours. He worked for Cudmore's Farm, next to the lace factory. He milked seven cows and fed 120 pigs twice a day every day of the week, for which he received 7s.0d. When he left school at 14 he went to work full time at the farm.

Mr Miller, the owner of the lace factory, also owned many of the houses in Derby and over Numbers 2 and 3 Corsor Street a bust of him was erected. The rent was 5s.6d. a week and Ernie's father, a lace maker, gave his wife £3 for housekeeping. As Ernie says, this was not a fortune with which to keep a family of 12 children.

The walls in the house were lathe and plaster, but not much plaster! Ernie told me they suffered from cockroaches and his mother's cure for these was an empty jam jar with a smearing of jam in it and half filled with water. When it was left overnight, to the children's delight, it would be full of insects the next morning.

At the top of Corsor Street were two washhouses where all the women from the 33 houses did their washing, with Monday being the usual washday. The children were sent to Cooks Carpentry Shop in Vicarage Lawn to collect bags of wood chippings and shavings for the fires under the six wash boilers. Afterwards, the washing was rinsed in galvanized troughs with Ricketts blue bags added to

❧ Derby ❧

Left: *Old Derby in 1948. The Boys Secondary Modern School is on the left and the entrance to the lace factory is on the right. The buildings beyond the Union Inn were cleared and in 2002 there is a roundabout on the Inner Relief Road.*

Right: *Union Street, Derby.*

Below: *A street plan of the Derby area, c.1930, drawn by George Laity from his memories of childhood days.*

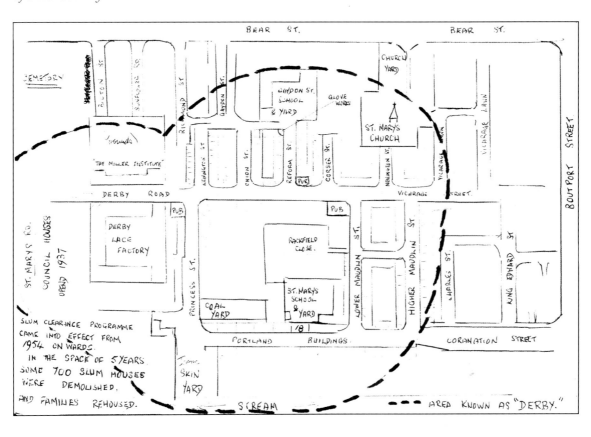

Above: *The Ovey family, 1914. Left to right, back row: Alice (who married William Lee, a builder), Ernest (who worked at the lace factory all his life), Jack (a carpenter and preacher at the Rackfield Mission), Mabel (who married Leonard Jones, a milkman), Bessie (who married and moved to London); seated: parents John and Sarah Ovey and Ern Ovey's father Frederick. This photograph was probably taken before Fred joined his regiment in France.*

Corser Street, c.1950.

A patriotic celebration for the children in Vicarage Street. The clock tower in the background belongs to the Miller Institute, later the Boys Seconday Modern School.

the 'whites'. The washing was hung out in the 20ft square drying area. No doubt this communal activity helped the women, as they could share their work and also their problems and family gossip.

Ernie also has strong memories of watching his mother ironing. She used two solid irons alternately, which stood on the Bodley cooking range to heat. The right temperature was gauged by the amount of sizzle produced when his mother spat on the heated side of the iron.

Ernie remembers his childhood in Derby as a happy time. No door was ever locked and everyone looked out for one another. Rent money was often left on the doorstep. If there was no one in, the gasman would let himself into the house and empty the meter, taking the money that was due and leaving the remainder on the table, along with the receipt.

Most people I have spoken to were aware that times were very difficult for their parents as money was in such short supply, but as children they did not have this worry which is no doubt why many of these stories can be retold light-heartedly. One such story is when the rent collector called and the young-ster who answered the knock at the door told him, 'Mother has gone up town.' Looking at the long curtain between the living-room and the kitchen the man answered, 'Next time she goes tell your Mother to take her feet with her!'

Alfred Fewings lived with his parents, Reggie and Florrie, and two brothers in York Place at the end of Princess Street. Florrie was one of the 15 children of a fish-erman on the River Taw. She was a washerwoman and had worked at the tuberculosis hospital in Castle Street. She died in 1999 aged 98 and still had a needle-sharp memory.

Florrie Fewings outside 21 York Place, Princess Street, in 1923. Alfred is in her arms, while her other son, Charlie, is standing next to their dog, Blackman.

Alfred's father, Reggie, suffered badly from injuries he received during the First World War. He worked for Barnstaple Corporation cleaning the streets. Often, after he had cleaned one particular street on his route the milk cart came round and the horse left a deposit. The lady of the house outside which this misdemeanor usually happened complained to the Council and Reggie was made very aware of this by his superiors. The next time the horse 'performed' Reggie returned to the street, scooped the offending matter onto his Corporation shovel, knocked on the lady's door and, when she opened it, deposited the said matter in her hallway with a suitable comment!

However, there was another side to Reggie. Alfred told me that during the Great Depression there were many tramps walking the roads, out of work and starving, and Reggie would feed them. At the back of their house was a wash-house with three boilers, one of which was used for making pigswill. Sometimes tramps would pick through the swill, trying to salvage something to eat. Alfred remembers that:

Father would produce a large jug of cocoa (no milk or sugar of course) and Mother made yeast cake or 'teddy-cake' to help fill them up. Father also ensured that of an evening there was hot water in the boilers so the tramps could have a wash.

One evening there came a knock at the door and Alfred was sent to answer it. It was pitch dark and when a hunched figure asked if it was correct that he could get a wash and drink here, Alfred naturally thought it was another unfor-tunate man down on his luck and called his father. Reggie came and directed the man round the back, telling him to help himself. It was then that the man revealed himself as Reggie's uncle, Sid Fewings, who lived at Sticklepath. He had heard of the good work his family was doing and had decided to check it out. Soon afterwards Uncle Sid made a donation to help with their charitable cause.

Alfred also told me that some people kept a pig in their backyard. After it had been fattened up it was slaughtered and butchered, then salted, stored and sold among the other residents.

Alfred recalled the man who lived at 1 Princess Street and had a shop around the corner. The house was a one-up, one-down and the shop-keeper lived upstairs and kept his donkey in the downstairs room!

Neighbourliness was echoed again when I spoke to Mary Stribling, who also lived in Princess Street. She said, 'You'd never be ill on your own. There was always someone to look after you.' She remembers everyone was trustworthy and it was quite usual to leave a note on the door saying, 'The key's under the mat'!

Other Derby memories are of the street parties and celebrations when all the streets were decorated and floral archways erected from one side to the other. On one occasion houses were painted patriotic

Right: *The Carpenters Arms in Vicarage Street, Derby, c.1950.*

Above: *Mr Offield and Charles Lock with daughters Betty and Mary (who later married Tom Stribling) outside Charles' pigeon house at 6 Princess Street.*

Left: *Derby bedecked for coronation celebrations.*

red, white and blue. People would come from miles around to see the decorations.

There were three public houses in Derby: the Carpenters Arms, the Union Inn and the Couriers Arms. Dai Morgan owned the Carpenters Arms. An amateur boxer, he promoted tournaments in the Pannier Market and once brought the heavyweight champion, Tommy Farr, to fight in Barnstaple. Mr Stephens, a man who was a keen pigeon fancier with a large handlebar moustache, ran the Union Inn. The licensee of the Couriers Arms was Mr Chugg.

Alfred said that at times Derby's reputation of being a rough place was deserved with three public houses which were open all day. On Saturday nights he would hang out of his bedroom window with his brother Charlie to await a fight. They were rarely disappointed. Perhaps this is why Derby got the reputation for policemen only going into the area in pairs!

After the First World War Fred and Ethel Laity returned to Ethel's home town and moved into Portland Buildings. Fred was a baker and found work at Southcombe's in Ilfracombe. He lodged there during the week and returned to Barnstaple at the weekends. His son, George, remembers Fred coming home, opening his suitcase and, along with his dirty washing, out would tumble swiss rolls and other goodies. In the 1920s Ethel, being an enterprising woman, got Fred to make a few pasties to sell at the

Mrs Rosie Cockram's shop on the corner of Lower Maudlin Street.

Couriers Arms. These became very popular and soon they had a roaring trade. From these small beginnings Ethel became a shopkeeper. They turned their front room into a store, selling sweets, cakes and general goods. This was not unusual in Derby where many a front room was converted into a small shop. However, Ethel went on to greater things and took on another business across town in Trinity Street, renting a lock-up shop where she sold sweets and cigarettes. One night, when all the shops were shut, news came that a furniture store in Trinity Street was on fire. With her eye to business Ethel rushed over there and opened up the shop, making a small fortune selling sweets and cigarettes to the fire watchers!

George Hewitt, who was born in 1919 and lived in Newington Street, told me that he first went to school when he was two years old. His mother, a war widow, became ill with rheumatic fever so Mrs Cousins, the head teacher of St Mary's School, agreed to let him join. (This was probably the Nursery School, as seen in the photograph on page 63, taken in the grounds of the Miller Institute.)

George told me of the many little shops in Derby, such as Mrs Kidwell's in Vicarage Street where she kept a large pile of dates on the counter. Also in Vicarage Street were shops owned by Miss May, Mrs Rosie Cockram and Miss Marsh, who always wore a high-collar blouse. She sold everything from toe-rag to dress material and sweets.

The Laitys of Derby

Left: *George and Ken Laity outside their house in Portland Buildings where their mother turned the front room into a shop.*

Above: *Playmates from Portland Buildings in 1927. Names include: R. Lawrence, M. Lawrence, R. Lawrence, L. Chapple, B. Featherstone, D. Lawrence, J. Philips, L. Richards, K. Laity and E. Philips.*

Below: *Ethel Laity outside her shop in Trinity Street, 1934.*

Above: *Fred Laity, 1927.*

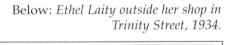

In Corsor Street was a lady who made wonderful faggots and in Newington Street Mr Butt had a front-room shop. Mr Hart sold coal from his backyard and after him was Mr Light, who was known for his 'finger weight' – he would break a piece of coal to get the exact weight.

Mr Graham Cudmore was a milkman, as was George Balment. George says the milk was sold around the streets from the back of a horse and cart. The warm milk was scooped out from a churn with a metal measure.

Most of the people I spoke to remember the passion for pigeon racing in Derby. When there was a race in progress everyone went out into the streets, waiting to catch a glimpse of the first pigeon to come home. A careful watch was kept for birds of prey and if spotted the cry would go up 'hawks in!' Women and children would then bang saucepan lids to scare away the predator.

Another area of old Barnstaple which was not only closely built but also close-knit was the streets in and around Queen Street. The entrance into Queen Street from Boutport Street was very narrow, as were the rest of the cobbled alleys and lanes within the maze of houses. Many of the families of men working on the river lived in the area behind the Square.

Alfred Drew (Abby to all who know him) was born in 1915 'somewhere in High Street' but soon moved to Azes Lane where he stayed until he was 43 years old. He has an absolute wealth of memories of old Barnstaple, which I will share with you during the course of the next few chapters.

The entrance to Azes Lane still stands on the Inner Relief Road opposite Alexandra Court, but there are only a few houses there now as the multi-storey car park has swallowed the rest of it. Abby says his house was two cottages which had been converted into one. There was no gas or electricity and cooking was done on a Bodley range. Lighting was by oil lamp and he remembers that they had to see their way to bed with candles.

Hardaway Head off Queen Street is now the entrance to the multi-storey car park. This thoroughfare emerged into a playing-area, opening out into Azes Lane. It is thought that at one time this was the direct route for leaving the town through Fort Hill then onwards via Newport to Exeter one way and Bristol or Taunton the other.

Iris Crook's mother died when Iris was only two years old and with her brother Ronald she went to live with her grandparents, James and Grace Parker, in Hardaway Head in 1920. They had ten children. Iris says she remembers that her Gran would wear a man's cap to cover her snow-white hair (although in the photo she loaned me Grace is without the cap). When Iris and Ronald went to live with their grandparents the house was so full that Iris slept on top of a metal sea-chest!

Michael Balman lived at Hardaway Head in the 1930s. His father, Walter, worked in the slaughterhouse by Long Bridge, where Halfords stands at the time of writing. His mother Daisy had the job of washing the animal skins in the River Taw and hanging them out to dry on poles beside the river. When Walter and his mates worked all night Daisy would get up at 4a.m. to collect beer from the White Lion in Silver Street and take it to the men for their early-morning refreshment.

Michael's memories of Hardaway Head are of a close-knit community. As with Derby, everyone looked after each other and everyone knew everybody's business. Some of the houses were so close together that from the upstairs windows you could shake hands with your neighbours across the road.

Left: Azes Lane, c.1950. The shop and two houses on the left still remain in 2002, along with the building on the right. Those in the background were demolished to make way for a multi-storey car park.

Right: *Azes Lane, c.1950.*

❧ Hardaway Head ❧

Hardaway Head.

Left: *Looking from Hardaway Head across Queen Street into Silver Street, c.1950.*

Grace Parker outside her home in Hardaway Head, 1925.

Left: *The crossroads at Queen Street, Trinity Street, Silver Street and Hardaway Head. This photograph shows houses at the top of Hardaway Head had been demolished. Later this became the site of a multi-storey car park.*

Left: *Belle Meadow, c.1940. The Shaddick family lived at Number 36 and their grandmother Mrs Lewis, who is on the right of the picture, lived at Number 38. The boy on the left is Monty Weeks and John Shaddick holds his grandmother's hand.*

Right: *A view of Lower Boutport Street, c.1925. The entrance to Queen Street is on the left. On the opposite side of the road is probably Mr Campbell with his ice-cream cart.* Photograph R.L. Knight.

Left: *Tom Gifford outside his shop on the corner of Queen Street and Hardaway Head, c.1950.*

Right: *Sanders Court prior to its demolition in 1949.*

There was a lady living in Hardaway Head who, every Sunday night when the Salvation Army came spreading the gospel by singing hymns, would curse them for all 'the noise they were making'. One Sunday her ultimate comment was the contents of her 'Gzunder' (chamber pot)! Needless to say the band of singers gave this location a miss for a few weeks!

After his National Service Michael worked for the Town Council as a carpenter and was in the workforce which demolished the Queen Street area – including his childhood home.

John Shaddick described Belle Meadow to me as a narrow street with small two-up, two-down cottages closely packed together. It could be entered either from Silver Street, through a narrow alleyway with a house built over the entrance, or from a pathway in Litchdon Street called Zions Place. This whole area became the Square car park, part of the new road system and the bus station.

John was the youngest of a family of five children. His mother Bessie died when he was just two. His grandmother and aunt only lived a few doors away, once again bringing together the extended family. John's family worked on the river (as described in Chapter Three) and John recalls his father keeping pigeons, rabbits and chickens in their backyard.

❧ Mapping the Area ❧

*A map of the area around the Square, Diamond Street, Wells Street and Silver Street.
It also shows Sanders Court.*

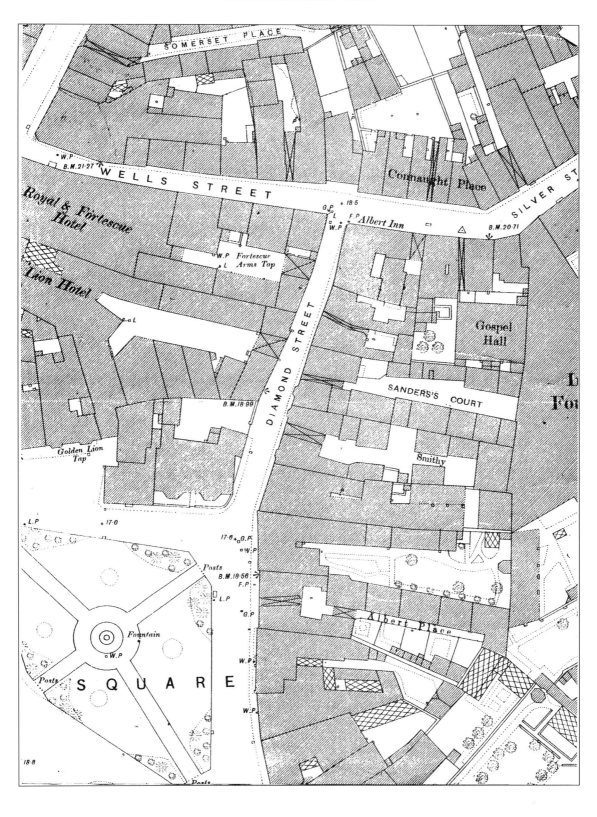

At Christmas his stepmother Hilda prepared fowls for Mr Gifford the butcher on the corner of Hardaway Head. The live birds would arrive for Hilda to kill, draw and pluck. John remembers the kitchen was always full of feathers at this time of year.

Other people who stand out in John's memory of that time were Mr Balment the cobbler and Fred Isaac, a slaughterman who also repaired shoes. Fred made soles out of old car tyres. John attended the Catholic School in Lower Church Street and his teacher, Miss Tout, called him 'Puss in Boots', as he always wore hobnail boots.

Abby Drew also told me of a Mr Campbell who lived in Belle Meadow and sold ice-cream from a handcart outside Catfords furniture shop opposite Queen Street *(see the photograph on p.56)*.

Abby was a milkman and came to know all the hidden parts of the town, for example Sanders Court, which was entered through an opening in Dymond Street. There were eight cottages in a row and across the courtyard were the wash-houses and toilets. Mrs Knott was one of the residents and she sold fish from a cart outside the Albert Hall in Boutport Street.

Sanders Court was bought by Bales Garage for use as workshops and Ian Bale, the grandson of the founder, was able to provide me with the photographs of the court before it was demolished.

Joan Webber told me that her husband Cyril was born above his parents' shop at 18 Silver Street. His father Ernie was a taxi driver and his mother Maud was an astute businesswoman who opened a café in Market Street and specialised in home-made bread and cakes.

An advertisement for Mrs Webber's café.

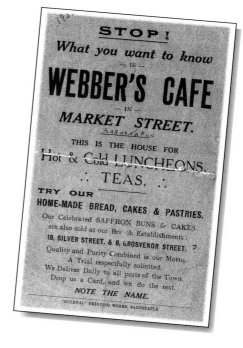

Above: *Cyril Webber outside his mother's shop at 18 Silver Street. They were both born here.*

Right: *Ernest and Maud Webber.*

Chapter Six

MEMORIES OF SCHOOL-DAYS

Private schools thrived alongside State education in Barnstaple in the first half of the last century. Most were small and had fewer than 50 youngsters, most giving their pupils a sound grounding in the three Rs – reading, writing and 'rithmetic.

Under the national school system, infant schools took children from as young as three to around eight years of age and junior schools took pupils up to the age of 14. Then the youngsters were sent out to work unless their parents could afford to send them to grammar school and/or a scholarship was awarded. That title meant something very different when Barnstaple's first grammar school was established over 300 years ago. The charity school at St Anne's Chapel in Paternoster Row gave a classical education to 30 scholars – all boys, of course! Poet John Gay of *The Beggars Opera* fame was one of them. When the chapel was refurbished in the 1980s for conversion into a small museum the wealth

of historical scholastic gems found under the floor-boards ranged from pencils to dried peas and shooters, dropped (or posted between the boards!) by scholars of times past.

Two other historic Barnstaple schools with names that have travelled down the years must be mentioned – the Alice Horwood School and the Blue Coat School. Alice was the wife of the town bene-factor, Thomas Horwood, and in 1659 she built a charity girls' school next to the almshouses in Church Lane, which were endowed by her husband. It took in 20 poor girls and taught them reading, knitting and sewing. Who better, then, than the girls of Alice Horwood to make the outfits which were provided twice yearly for the 50 boys at the charity Blue Coat School in rooms above the North Gate, at the far end of the High Street. The girls (who also got new outfits twice a year) used local woollen cloth known as Barnstaple Baize.

Blue Coat School, North Walk.

❧ Blue Coat School & Art School ❧

Right: *Blue Coat School's headmaster, Mr Woodhouse, and his class, c.1910. The boy in the white jumper is thought to be George Wickham and his brother Fred is next to Mr Woodhouse in the second row. Both boys were killed in the First World War.*

Left: *The High Street, c.1935. The building beside the two ladies on the left was the Literary and Scientific Institution, later known as the Art School.* Photograph R.L. Knight.

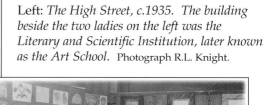

Right: *An exhibition of work at the Art School in 1920.*

Blue Coat School pupils in 1957.

When the North Gate was demolished a purpose-built school was erected just around the corner in North Walk. Over the years it became co-educational and then part of the State system and when it amalgamated with Pilton Church of England School in 1969 it had been educating Barnstaple's children for 250 years. The old building was pulled down and became a shoppers' car park.

Former Blue Coat pupils I've spoken to remember a certain headmaster in the 1920s named Mr Woodhouse. He was, recalls George Hewitt, a red-headed Irishman with a temper to match and a heavy hand. Others echo this story, except the hair colour changes down the years to white!

When Raymond Wickham joined the Blue Coat School in 1940, his first impression of his new head-master was of Neville Chamberlain, the Prime Minister the country had just sacked! Raymond's mother believed that one of her children should be a musician and as he was the youngest and his siblings had shown no interest in the art the task fell to him in the form of the violin. Being presented with the instru-ment one day he asked his mother, 'What's this for?' 'You're having music lessons. Report to Mr Woodhouse at 2 o'clock,' his mother informed him. At the appointed time Raymond duly presented himself and his violin to Mr Woodhouse's study. Inside were two older pupils and another man. The headmaster looked Raymond up and down and told him to get his instrument and 'Show us what you can do.' Raymond took the violin from its case, put it to his shoulder and held the bow with the other hand, which was the total sum of his musical ability. The headmaster roared 'Play', and Raymond asked, 'How?' 'Are you a beginner?' demanded Mr Woodhouse. When Raymond answered in the affirmative the teacher yelled, 'We don't do beginners – go away.' This ended Raymond's career as a violinist!

Keith James recalls that at lunchtimes they would play a form of netball in the playground nearest Tuly Street. A metal ring without a net was affixed to the wall and opposite it in the playground they placed a netball stand. He says the rules were more or less the same as netball, only the pitch was really too small. He remembers that his team was called the 'Bulldogs'.

It is here that mention must be made of the Literary and Scientific Institution, which opened in 1845 at 42 High Street (the National Westminster Bank stands there now). One of its main benefactors was William Rock, who provided 600 books for the library and £100 a year for students who could not afford the fees. In 1888 it was moved to the Athenaeum, secured by William Rock with an endowment of £12,000. For 100 years this also housed the County Library.

The school in the High Street now became the Barnstaple Art, Science and Commercial School. Norman Brooks entered these portals of learning in 1943 at the age of 13 to start a three-year junior building course. He told me the uniform was maroon and included a cap with the Devon coat of arms on it. From the entrance hall a long corridor lined with Roman busts on plinths went the whole length of the building and opened into a yard at the back, through which was access to Green Lane. Norman's classroom was upstairs and from there he could look down on the High Street into a café oppo-site, which had a large stuffed bear in the window.

During the Second World War the students were issued with coloured counters which they used to purchase lunch at the British Restaurant in the Albert Hall, one of a chain of eateries set up by the Government in those days of food shortages and rationing.

The Art School, as it was known, was the early version of the North Devon College. After 1945 the Technical School had classes there and at Pilton, in buildings that had been used by the Army during the war (where the Fire Station stands at the time of writing). In 1953 the new Technical College was opened on its present site at Sticklepath. Keith James was the first head boy and he recalls taking part in the opening ceremony.

The Art School continued to be used for lessons after the Technical School was relocated. As a pupil of Pilton Primary School I remember that in the mid 1950s, when our school was over-subscribed with pupils, the senior classes had to go to the Art School for lessons. It was fun watching the street below from our birds-eye viewing point of the classroom windows. I also remember the whack of the slipper when caught hanging too far out of the window!

I have been told of many small private schools that existed in the early part of the twentieth century. John and Peggy Huxtable's first school was run by Miss Mew. This was at the top of Fort Street and had about 30 pupils and two classroom assistants. John told me that Miss Mew was very strict but gave them a sound basis for their future education. John's next school was Miss Wright's in Ebberly Lawn; two sisters ran this. His parents soon removed him from this

In 1967 the four girls fulfilled a promise and met for a celebration tea party. Left to right: *Mrs Nelly Cheriton, Miss Dorothy Down, Mrs Winny Becklake (née Ashton) and Mrs Eva Heywood.*

Pupils of Miss Lyle's private school in a Christmas play held at the Parish Church Rooms in 1930.
Photograph R.L. Knight.

Above: *Miss Inkson's Addiscombe School, Boutport Street, c.1907. In this group are the four girls who promised to meet again in their seventieth year.*

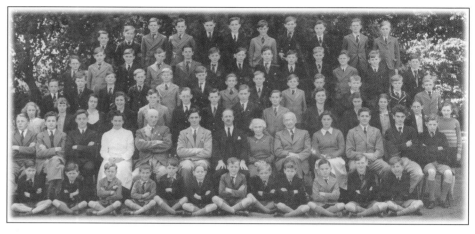

Right: *Belmont College pupils and staff, 1942.*

establishment, as they feared the discipline was not firm enough. Ellerslie Boys School followed, a private school in a large house on the Ellerslie estate near Bickington which had 28 pupils. It later became Belmont College when a school of that name was evacuated to Barnstaple in 1940 from war-torn London.

Michael James and Sidney Hillman, who were both wartime pupils, still attend the school reunions. Michael said there were about 50 boys at the school in four classrooms and the headmaster, Mr Heffer, 'was a really nice gentleman.' The uniform was black with a gold star badge on the blazer and cap, and the school was well known for its sporting prowess.

James Sanders recalls the little school he attended at the top of Park Lane, which was run by Miss Lyle. She was the sister of Sydney Harper, the author and owner of a large bookshop in Butcher's Row. Brother and sister were also musically artistic and gave poetry and song recitals.

Michael Bromley, whose family ran a well-known High Street restaurant and bakery, told me that he went to Miss Macmillan's Kindergarten School, which was in a lane off the Strand opposite the bus station.

Sheila Gear told me a lovely story about her mother Winnie Becklake, who was the youngest daughter of Lawrence and Polly Ashton who owned Ashton's grocery shop in the High Street. Winnie attended Miss Inkson's Addiscombe School in Boutport Street. On their last day at school Winnie and three of her best friends made a pact to meet again and celebrate their seventieth birthdays. In 1967 Winnie, Nellie Cheriton, Dorothy Down and Eva Heywood kept their promise and had a celebratory tea.

Monica Wonnacott, who lived on a farm at Bishops Tawton, also has many school-time memories. When she was three years old her mother sent her to stay with different families in Newport, so that she could attend Cyprus Terrace School. Her mother Ruby Jackman had a milk round in Barnstaple and wanted Monica to attend the Newport School, but the family lived outside the school's catchment area. Mrs Jackman approached several of her Newport customers, which led to Monica's stay with families such as the Rhinds in Norfolk Terrace, the Normans in Clinton Road and her mother's cousin Mrs Warwick. Monica recalls the photographer coming to the school to take the yearly pictures. The class was neatly seated and, to keep their attention for the time it took to capture their innocent faces, the photographer told them to 'Watch for the birdie.' Monica, being inquisitive by nature, decided to investigate where the bird was kept and got up to get a better view of the inside of the camera just as the shutter clicked.

❧ *Infant Schools* ❧

Left: *St Mary's infants in the grounds of the Miller Institute in the 1920s. Those pictured include: Bert Offield (on the left), Jackie Darch and his sister, Miss Cousins (the teacher), Betty Fewings (right) and George Laity (far right).*

Right: *Pupils of Cyprus Terrace School, 1905. Cecil Bale, whose father owned the Trafalgar Cycle Works in Newport, is pictured third from the left in the front row.*

Left: *The infant class of Cyprus Terrace School, 1931. Left to right, back row: Micky Rawlings, Harold Down, ?, Ivor Glasson, Eric Richards, Bobby Knight; centre: Mary Berry, Jean Smale, Ivy Biddle, Monica Jackman (who stood up to watch 'the Birdie'), Margaret Smale, Jean Sluman; front row: Desmond Jewell, ? Berry, Reggie Allen, ?, ?, ?.*

Right: *St Mary's School, 1932. Betty Lake is pictured to the right of the desk with No. 3 on it. Other pupils in this group include Colin Combes, Tom Fetherstone, Ken Smith, Len Pickard, Len Richards, Jim Bower, Betty Fewings and George Laity.*

❧ The Girls' National School ❧

Above: *Empire Day celebrations at the Girls' National School, North Walk, in 1933.*

Left: *Miss Rose, the headmistress of the Girls' National School, is pictured seated with Miss Rudd to her left, in 1929.*

Below: *A drill display in the playground of the National School, 1936. The houses in the background are in Castle Street and back on to the Cattle Market.*

Other infant schools in the town were associated with churches – the Parish Church School, Pilton School, Holy Trinity School and St Mary Magdalene School. George Laity went to St Mary's when he was three and remembers that on warm summer days the nursery class was taken to the Miller Institute gardens opposite the lace factory, where they would lie on portable cots and have their afternoon sleep.

Pupils who attended St Mary's usually moved up to the Wesleyan School, better known as Gaydon Street School. Michael Locke, who went to this school in 1949, remembers teachers such as the Misses Bond, Husband, Power and Carter along with their male counterparts, Eggleton, Chugg and Driver. He has fond memories of two huge sycamore trees in the school grounds which took five children with hands linked to circle the trunks.

The Girls' National School was on North Walk by the entrance to the Cattle Market and later became the Telephone Exchange. Information about this teaching establishment has been nothing but complimentary. Joy Browne (née Parsley) had a great deal of praise for the headmistress, Miss Rose, and teachers the Misses Cutland, Husband and Rundle. Joy remembers a schools' poetry competition held at the Forester's Hall and she was in the team that won the competition. Joy told me that Miss Rose took the winning group of five girls to the Regal Cinema then to her home in Ilfracombe, where they had fresh salmon sandwiches for tea.

The school obviously had a great interest in the theatrical talents of its pupils as I was shown photographs of productions, many of them staged in the playground beside the Cattle Market.

When the education system changed in 1939 the pupils of the national schools who were nearing 14 had to transfer to the new secondary modern schools. The girls went to Ashleigh Road School and the boys to the school in Vicarage Street. One nickname it had was 'Mr Heppenstall's School for Young Gentlemen' (or a less complimentary name for gentlemen!) Mr Heppenstall was this school's first headmaster. He was involved with several organisations in the town, such as St John's Ambulance Brigade and the Barnstaple Swimming Club. Before the swimming baths were built in Rock Park he taught the boys to swim in the River Taw. However, most of the 'young gentlemen' I have spoken to remember this teacher for his corporal punishment rather than his teaching skills. Mr Heppenstall had previously been the headmaster of Ashleigh Road School. Abby Drew, who was a pupil, told me that from the age of seven he did an early morning milk round which often made him late for school and this always resulted in him receiving 'Six of the Best'.

On Wednesdays the boys had what today would be called 'work experience', with the choice of gardening or carpentry. Gardening was taught on a plot of land behind the school and the pupils grew their own vegetables. Abby was given the job of tending the kidney beans. He had to harvest them and take them to Smallridge's the greengrocers, which was then at the bottom of the Strand. When Mr Heppenstall caught Abby and some of his mates eating the carrots they had been sent to sort in the garden shed they were charged 9d. for each carrot and received several whacks from the cane.

Above: *Mr Heppenstall teaching boys from Ashleigh Road School to swim in the River Taw, 1921.*

Below: *The headmaster and his pupils sitting to attention on the banks of the Taw.*

Left: *Ashleigh Road Boys football team who beat the Blue Coat Boys 1–0 to win the cup in 1922. In the photograph can be seen: Mr Morgan, F. Popham, Mr Heppenstall, C. Tunner, Preston Denny, Bunny Short, Mr Chugg, Tom Somerfield, Frank Chapple, Horace Steer, W. Wakley, M. Williams, Bill Williams (who scored the winning goal) and E. Mock.*

Edward Blacksell, headmaster of the Boys' Secondary Modern School.

Soon after the move to Vicarage Street a young gym teacher named Edward Blacksell arrived at the Boys' Secondary Modern School and following wartime service with the RAF he returned to become the headmaster. He is remembered with respect by teachers and pupils alike. I am told it was his intention to rid the pupils of their feelings of failure at not passing the 11-plus examination and give them a sense of achievement. You would expect no more from a man who had been Liaison Officer to MacIndoe's Guinea Pigs (the wartime aircrews that suffered terribly disfiguring burns). His encouragement and support helped these men for many years after the war.

Michael Locke was a pupil of this school in the mid 1950s and has a clear recollection of teachers such as Mr Uglow, who taught English and was also a cricket fanatic. If the boys finished their work before the end of the lesson he would allow them to listen to the cricket reports on the wireless. Mr Uglow also taught evening classes in electronics and helped the boys build a wireless. There was also Mr Gisby the metalwork teacher, who played the violin and if lessons finished before the allotted time would treat them to a classical piece on his fiddle.

Michael also told me of the time in Mr Davis' gardening class when some chicks hatched which, as far as Michael can recall, was the only lesson in which they were taught about the 'birds and the bees'!

As far as the Girls' Secondary Modern School is concerned I can speak from my own experience. In 1958, as a young girl coming in from a small village school at Marwood, I found it awesome. The main red-brick building held five classrooms, a library and school hall, with classrooms scattered around in wooden huts or pre-fab buildings. Another classroom was held in the Territorial Army building next door. We were forever putting on macs and coats to go from one lesson to another. This led to unsatisfied staff and a disjointed education for the girls. I left as soon as possible, at 15 years old.

A brand new school opened in Chaddiford Lane a year later where I'm sure the conditions were far more suitable for the education of students. Frank Kidwell became the caretaker. He told me there were about 600 pupils and he had seven lady cleaners. In 1970, when it became a co-educational comprehensive school with Edward Blacksell as its head, there were at least 1,500 pupils and Frank had 21 cleaners on his staff.

The last (at least, in name) Barnstaple Grammar School was built at Newport above Rock Park in 1910 and is today the Park School. A brochure produced for parents in 1915 underlines the way in which not just education but the whole social fabric has been

Mr Tom Long taking the roll-call of pupils before they depart on an educational cruise to the Mediterranean on the SS Devonian *in 1967. Some of the boys in this group are:* Philip Dymond, Paul Dymond, Pip Denning, Chris Stacey, ? Stevens, Ian Rose, John Barthram, Chris Simmonds, Peter Salter, Martin Spencer, Andy James, Mr Gordon Ridd. *Photograph used by kind permission of* North Devon Journal Herald.

Left: Grammar School Football Team, 1918–19. Frederick Critchley, Senior Master at the Grammar School is the man with the moustache in the back row.

Below: The Grammar School, now Park School.

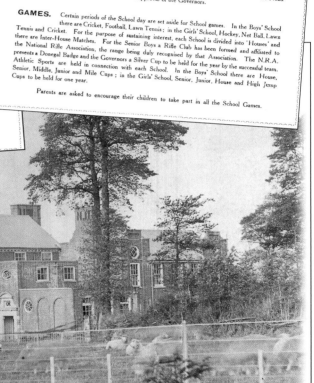

BOARDERS. By the consent of the Governors, arrangements to board Boys by the Term or Week, can be made with Mr. W. O. Turner, B.A., 23 Hill's View, Barnstaple, by an interview either with him, or with the Head Master. The Fees, which are exclusive of Tuition Fees, are as follows :—under 13, Terminal, £6 : 6 : 0, Weekly, £5 : 5 : 0 ; over 13, Terminal, £8 : 8 : 0, Weekly, £7 : 7 : 0. Information as to Terms for the boarding of Girls can be obtained from the Head Mistress. Boarding arrangements require the approval of the Governors.

GAMES. Certain periods of the School day are set aside for School games. In the Boys' School there are Cricket, Football, Lawn Tennis ; in the Girls' School, Hockey, Net Ball, Lawn Tennis and Cricket. For the purpose of sustaining interest, each School is divided into 'Houses' and there are Inter-House Matches. For the Senior Boys a Rifle Club has been formed and affiliated to the National Rifle Association, the range being duly recognised by that Association. The N.R.A. presents a Donegal Badge and the Governors a Silver Cup to be held for the year by the successful team. Athletic Sports are held in connection with each School. In the Boys' School there are House, Senior, Middle, Junior and Mile Cups ; in the Girls' School, Senior, Junior, House and High Jump Cups to be held for one year.

Parents are asked to encourage their children to take part in all the School Games.

ADMISSION. Application for Forms of Admission to the School should be made to the Heads of the respective Schools, or to the Clerk of the Governors, and be returned with a testimonial as to character. A Health Certificate, signed by a parent or guardian, must be brought on the first day of each term as a necessary condition of admission for that term. Pupils must not be absent except in case of illness. A Pupil returning to School after absence must bring a note stating the reason for that absence. In cases of contagious or infectious illness the Head Master or Mistress must be informed at once, and the parent or guardian will receive a special Health Form which must be signed by a Doctor certifying that the Pupil has recovered from the illness before the Pupil will be admitted having recovered from that illness. Pupils must wear the School Cap or a Straw Hat in accordance with the regulation of their respective schools. All Pupils must be in their places on the first day of the School Term.

REPORTS, &c. Attested Reports are sent to Parents at the close of each term showing progress of each Pupil. The School year begins in September, and is divided into three terms of about 13 weeks each. The holidays consist of about 3 weeks at Christmas, Easter, and 7 in Summer.

The School Hours are normally from 9-0 a.m. to 12-40 p.m., and from 2-10 p.m. 4-10 p.m. Saturday is a whole holiday.

Homework, graduated according to Form, is set throughout the School, and it is essential to the success of a Pupil's School life that homework should have the first claim to attention in the evening. The discipline in the Schools is in the hands of the Head Master and Head Mistress respectively.

transformed over the past century. Boys and girls were taught in separate buildings. The girls had a special room for domestic studies while the boys honed their DIY skills – and often their future careers – in a manual workshop. The wide curriculum included English, arithmetic, chemistry, physics, French, German, algebra, euclid (geometry), singing, physical drill, nature study, Latin and Greek. Religious instruction was given within the principles of the Christian faith. But that is not all! Boys could also take shorthand classes for 3s.6d. a term, while girls could have dancing lessons for 10s.6d. (The

social graces seem to have been highly prized, judging by the disparity in cost!) Basic tuition fees for pupils aged from nine to 12 were £2.10s. per term, while seniors' fees were £3.3s. per term. To encourage parents to choose the school, if their children joined before the age of 11 the term fee stayed at the lower rate for their entire education.

There was one practical difficulty in those days – getting to school from outlying communities. It was therefore necessary to provide weekly boarding for pupils from outside the town, which was an extra expense for parents.

Form 3A of Barnstaple Girls' Grammar School, 1946. Left to right, back row: Phyllis Barrow, Mice Mitchell, Mary Short, Diana London, Beryl Parsley, Sally Bushen, Pricilla Harding, Valerie Gould; centre: Ruth Morrish, Christine Wyborn, Fay ?, ?, ?, Margaret Gubb, Norah Greenslade, ?, Margaret Brough, Patsy Chugg; front row: Rosemary Everett, Elizabeth Lake, Vanessa Agutter, Miss E. Davies, Madame Jamart, Miss Watson, Sheila Ridd, ?, Vida Wonnacott.

Nora Maynard, a lady in her 98th year, tells me that she lived at Atherington and won a scholarship to the grammar school. Early on a Monday morning she would walk more than a mile to the railway station at Umberleigh and catch the train to Barnstaple. On Fridays her brother took her home by pony and trap after going to Barnstaple Market. During the week Nora boarded with a family in Bear Street.

Several years later the girls' school got its own boarding-house in Riversvale House on the corner of Litchdon Street, a property which is now part of the NHS Healthcare Trust. Monica Jackman from Bishops Tawton lodged there and recalls that when the school matron was a patient in the North Devon Infirmary opposite, the girls went across to the porter's lodge every day, where a notice was posted on the state of seriously ill patients. She also told me of the occasion during the Second World War when the girls were picnicking on Saunton Beach and saw a soldier mis-throw a grenade, which badly injured his arm. The girls 'adopted' him and watched his progress on the notice-board.

My thanks go to Enid Critchley who loaned me the booklet from the grammar school's early years. Her husband Frederick was a much-respected master there from 1914 until 1953.

Girls' Grammar School magazine.

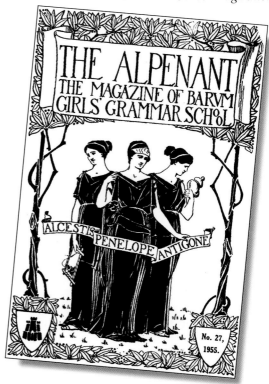

Chapter Seven

INDUSTRIOUS BARUM

Sand being unloaded from a boat into Rawle, Gammon & Baker's yard.

The industries mostly associated with Barnstaple are those which provided the majority of work over the past two centuries: lace and glove manufacturers, potteries, cabinet makers, wood and wool merchants and iron foundries. For some of them the basic materials were available on the doorstep, such as clay for pottery, wool for sheepskin products and skins for some of the gloves. The others had to import their raw materials.

Wood Merchants

The firm of Rawle, Gammon & Baker was established in 1850 and still stands on the same site by Rolle Bridge, although plans are afoot as I write to move to a more accessible site at Pottington. It began with wood but today, of course, is a huge general builders merchants.

William Gammon was a builder who lived in Lower Maudlin Street, where he also had his yard. He is reputed to have built the house that became the Athenaeum, as well as St Mary's Church and the National Provincial Bank on the corner of the High Street and Cross Street (now a photographic shop). Samuel Rawle was a lathe maker who also owned the Rolle Arms alehouse that stood where the Rolle Quay Inn stands at the time of writing. The two men formed a partnership to import logs to convert into timber for the building trade. Their first office was in the cottage next door to the Rolle Arms and on the marshy ground opposite was a sawpit where two men, one working at the top and one on the other end of a saw down in the pit, would convert the large logs into workable planks. It was hard, thirsty work so the proximity of the Rolle Arms must have been an advantage. The sawyers could convert 150 feet of softwood in one day (modern machines cope with this amount in 90 seconds).

❧ *Generations of RGB Owners* ❧

Right: *Frederick Baker with his wife. Charlie Bennett is the coachman.*

Below: *William Pyke Gammon.*

Bottom: *William Gammon junr enjoying a picnic with his family.*

Right: *William Gammon, founder of Rawle, Gammon & Baker.*

✌ Generations of RGB Owners ❧

Above: *James Henry Gammon in the doorway of the Rawle, Gammon & Baker Rolle Street offices.*

Inset: *Major Jack Gammon.* Photograph R.L. Knight.

Right: *Richard John Gammon (known as Young John).*

Left: *Roger Isaac.*

Right: *Giles Isaac (right), the current Chairman and Managing Director of the firm. He is seated with Kevin Fenlon, the Chief Executive.*

Above: *Manhandling a length of timber into the storage sheds.*

Above: *Unloading timber at Castle Quay, which was then taken by horse and cart to the Rolle Street yard, 1920.*

Left: *Bob Ridd and a workman sawing timber.*

From 1853 boats were chartered to bring the wood from Canada, Poland, Scandinavia and Africa. Vessels unloaded at Appledore, where the logs were chained together in rafts and floated up the River Taw to Pottington Marsh. There were difficulties in moving the wood from Appledore to Barnstaple, so in 1861 Rawle and Gammon bought the *Ariadne*, a three-masted sailing ship. Her first cargo from St John's in Newfoundland was prob-ably brought right into Rolle Quay. The next trip was less successful as she grounded on the rocks off Appledore. The repairs cost £500. Now they were shipowners, Rawle and Gammon had to find cargoes for the outward journeys and in 1863 they advertised the *Ariadne* as an emigrant ship for its voyage to Quebec. Passages were offered at £5 a head. She left from Rolle Quay for the six-week voyage with 15 local men as crew and returned with a full load of timber.

In 1878 William Gammon died. The following year his three sons were made partners, along with Samuel Rawle's son-in-law, Frederick Baker, and the firm became Rawle, Gammon & Baker. Baker had been a journalist and would sit at his desk in the morning with the newspaper fixed in front of him – he never held it. He had to know all the day's news

before the customers came in! He also had a string and pulley set up through the window so that when he pulled it the foreman was summoned to his office. Samuel Rawle died in 1881.

The company built cottages for employees, new offices, a mill and drying sheds in Rolle Street. In 1893 the third generation, in the form of William Gammon, joined the company and went around North Devon on a pedal cycle carrying on the firm's business.

The unfortunate car that ended up over the railings at High Wall, Sticklepath.

In 1915 Frederick Baker died and his son was killed on active service, ending the Rawle and Baker connections with the business. In 1922, after his military service, William John Gammon (known as Jack) joined the firm. He was somewhat absent-minded and once he forgot to engage the handbrake on his car when it was parked outside a house on High Wall, Sticklepath. As the photograph shows the car ended up impaled on the railings.

The business expanded in 1932 when it opened a branch at Bideford and during the Second World War the yards were used to store timber for the war effort. In 1949 Jack Gammon's son Richard John (known as young John) joined the business along with his cousin Roger Isaac. Richard was a man of great foresight and brought calculators into the firm when they were first on the market. He was also a keen jazz enthusiast and

S.S. HERNIA. Discharging Archangel Cargo for Rawle, Gammon and Baker.
Barnstaple, July, 1928.

A postcard view of the Archangel *unloading timber at Castle Quay. This postcard would have been sent out to customers informing them that their goods were ready for collection.*

Ex-Second World War gun carriers purchased by Rawle, Gammon & Baker to transport the timber being delivered to Castle Quay.

brought jazz bands to play in the town. Unfortunately he suffered from ill health and died before his father in 1975. Roger Isaac carried on at the head of the firm and in 2002 his son Giles continues the family business, which operates not only from Barnstaple but also Bideford, Chapleton, Exeter, Launceston, Paignton, Holsworthy and Wiveliscombe.

My thanks go to Giles Isaac, the present Chairman and Managing Director of RGB, and his father Roger for allowing me to help myself to the family photographs. Also I am grateful for the loan of a manuscript of a talk given by Miss Phyllis Gammon to the Devonshire Association in the 1980s about the company.

Cabinet makers

The longest surviving and best known of the cabinet makers is Shapland and Petter, now known as Leaderflush & Shapland, on the banks of the River Taw on the far side by Long Bridge. After more than a century there, it is to relocate away from the congestion of the town in 2002.

Henry Shapland, a cabinet maker, set up his company in one room at Raleigh Woollen Mill, Pilton and later moved to Bear Street. Henry Petter, an accountant, joined the business and in 1864 they bought the original factory where Shapland had first worked. It was here that the world-renowned business of Shapland and Petter's Raleigh Works was born. Then, in 1888 the factory burned down and was rebuilt on the Long Bridge site. This allowed easier access for ships unloading their timber.

Henry Shapland died in 1909, two years after Henry Petter, and in 1924 Shapland and Petter merged with the Barnstaple Cabinet Works.

I spoke to Clifford Boddy, who spent 50 years with Shapland and Petter. His father, Bertie, had started work at the Barnstaple Cabinet Works, known as 'the new firm', at the bottom of Newport and later

moved to Shapland's when it took over the business.

Clifford started work in 1933 with a five-year apprenticeship. This had some severe restrictions, such as not being allowed to marry until he reached the age of 21! There was a great deal of craftsmanship in their work and they specialised in furniture for banks, churches and liners such as the *Canberra*. Later, the company went into manufacturing doors and door sets, mostly for hospitals.

Roy Braund, who came from Bideford, joined Shapland's at the age of 14 and trained to be a cabinet maker and joiner. Roy told me that there were at least 30 apprentices at any one time and he recalls Reginald Northcote, who was in charge of them, as a good teacher and kindly man who supplied treats for his lads, such as mince pies at Christmas. Like Clifford before him, Roy had an affinity for wood which his headmaster at Bideford had recognised and invited him to join a woodwork class out of school hours. Roy also had to attend Saturday morning classes at the factory. Another memory sparked off by our conversation was of the canteen where Cyril Brooks, an ex-Army cook, ran a very successful kitchen and Roy still recalls mouthwatering delights, such as Cyril's raspberry buns and sugary jam doughnuts. After Cyril left the canteen was run by Mrs Hughes, who produced laver (edible seaweed) for a lunchtime meal which wasn't such a hit with the men!

As a young lad fresh out of school Roy had to travel to work on the bus until he had saved enough money to buy his first motorbike. This landed him and other young apprentices in hot water when they took to their motorcycles at lunch-times and used the town centre as a race circuit, up the High Street and down Boutport Street where, at the lower end near the cinema, they could open up the throttle and do 'wheelies', causing a great deal of noise. Complaints from people soon had these young men banned from the town during their lunch break.

❧ Cabinet Production ❧

Left: *Postcard sketch of Raleigh Cabinet Works. This was destroyed by fire in 1888.*

Right: *The replacement factory of Shapland and Petter's Raleigh Works, built on the Sticklepath side of the Long Bridge.*

Left: *After the factory relocated beside the estuary it made timber delivery so much easier.*

Right: *Shapland and Petter craftsmen at work on a screen for a bombed church in South Devon, 1952. Left to right: Stan Mills, Harold Fice, Clifford Boddy, Mr Roberts, Alfie Karwatt Veneer; front row: Cyril Higgins, Fred Hill.*

Left: *A bar being made for a liner in the joinery room. The third man from the left is Percy Hunt, the man at the back on the right is Mr Priscott, and the man on the far right is Mr Courtney. Photograph used by kind permission of Museum of Barnstaple and North Devon.*

Whilst showing me the photograph of the joinery shop Roy told me about the process of glueing the wood together with Scotch glue. It was made from animal bones and had a highly unpleasant odour. Each man had his own glue pot, which was prepared in 'Hells Kitchen', so named because he said it was as hot as Hades! The glue started as a solid lump and once at the correct consistency was kept in a glue kettle. Six pots stood in a trough, which was supplied with steam through a water jacket around the outside. You had to work fast as the glue set quickly. All the relevant parts had to be at the ready before you collected your pot from the trough. Another use for the trough was at mid-morning break, when the men would hang their tea bottles around the water jacket to enable the steam to warm them.

Part of Roy's work was to make or modify door handles for furniture and he had to visit Curry's smithy behind the Police Station in Castle Street. Miles Curry was the blacksmith and Alec his brother was the accounts man. Roy said that when he had to go upstairs to the office Alec would be seated on a high chair at his desk in surroundings that came straight out of a Dickens novel. Everything was brown with dust and covered with cobwebs, but Alec had a needle-sharp recall of all his accounts. Miles had a huge store of locks and equipment and if he did not have the required piece in stock he would make it at the forge.

Potters

Clay suitable for pottery making was plentiful in and around Barnstaple, so it is not surprising that the town was home to some extremely talented art potters. Barnstaple Literary and Scientific Institute (later known as the Art School) in the High Street was a great asset to the artistic in the community. It was here that Charles Brannam was encouraged by William Rock, founder of the institute, to perfect his designs. Thomas Brannam had been a potter with the Rendell Potteries in the town from the 1830s. His son Charles, who was born in 1855, joined him in the Litchdon Street pottery at the age of just 13. Charles received his art training by working with his father at the pottery and with his brother-in-law photographer William Briton at his High Street studio as well as his evening classes at the institute.

A kiln once used by Brannam's in their Litchdon Street Pottery now preserved in the grounds of Brannam's Medical Centre.

Thomas Parsley at work with his potter's wheel.

After ten years perfecting his skills with throwing, firing, mixing glazes and designing he persuaded his father to let him take over the pottery in Litchdon Street. Here in 1879 the birth of Brannam's Art Pottery, more commonly known as Barum Ware, took place. Although Charles Brannam was very much a working owner he also employed some very talented designers and potters. For further information on this subject I recommend a visit to the North Devon Museum.

Joy Browne told me of her father, Thomas Parsley, who lived in St George's Road, Yeo Vale and from an early age was a potter at Brannam's. During the First World War he served with the Devonshire Regiment in France and afterwards returned to Brannam's. Joy remembers with pride her visits to the pottery, watching her father at work at the potter's wheel. A young lad prepared the balls of clay and she watched in awe as he threw the clay onto the wheel and her father magically produced a beautifully rounded vase. She also recalled the 'secret' blue dye they used and how he made a vase in this blue colour, which had a dragon fashioned on the front in wonderful shades of blue and green.

It cannot go unmentioned that while Brannam's is still in existence there have been other renowned potteries and art potters in and around Barnstaple. Alexander Lauder, a trained architect, designed the Gliddon and Squire building which stands in Tuly Street with its ornate brick exterior frieze. From his pottery at Pottington he made ornamental bricks and tiles and the best example of his work could be seen at his home at Ravelin Manor. Lauder was a popular man and was Mayor of the town for two years. He was also an instructor at the Art Institute and Charles Brannam was one of his students.

William Baron joined Brannam's in 1884 and was renowned for his natural designs featuring birds, fish and flowers. He left there to work at the Fishley pottery at Fremington and later set up his own pottery at Mill Road, giving his own work the brand name of Baron Ware. After his death in 1937 Brannam's bought the business.

The original Brannam pottery, with its distinctive, highly collectable designs, is much sought after. At the time of writing, at their new premises on the outskirts of the town, Brannam's mainly specialise in terracotta ware, which is distributed worldwide.

Lace makers

There were several lace factories in the town in the 1800s. One was opposite the North Devon Infirmary, on ground which was later incorporated into Rock Park, and another was at Raleigh. John Boden, who hailed from Derby, built one on land at the end of Vicarage Lane, which in those days was some distance from the town. This became known as the Derby lace factory.

Streets of houses for the workers soon sprang up on the land between the town and the factory and it became generally known as Derby. In 1828 John Miller from Loughborough became the new owner of the factory and following his death his three sons carried on the business until 1903. The factory is still in existence today. It is an imposing building, as are two other surviving properties associated with the Miller family. One is Gorwell House, which was built as the family home by John Miller, and the other was the Miller Institute, now Yeo Valley School. This stands opposite the factory and was built by Alfred Miller (one of John's sons) as an institute for the benefit of the lace-factory workers and their families. Workers could attend evening classes and enjoy the surrounding gardens, bowls green and football pitch.

Gorwell House, an imposing Georgian villa, was built in the early 1830s high above the town, with breathtaking views of the river estuary. This would only have been a short carriage drive from his factory but was far removed from the dingy streets in which John Miller's workers lived. Today this is the home of sculptress Vanessa Marston and her GP husband John, who is not only a talented musician but also a keen gardener. This is helpful as he has five acres of garden which he opens to the public several times a year.

My research took me to visit Alfred Fewings, who worked at the factory for 40 years and became the mill manager. He told me that the machines were lubricated with graphite, as oil could not be used near the lace. The graphite, however, would make the lace very dirty, so it all had to be washed after the process of curtain making was complete. Lace repairing was sent out to women in their homes. Alf showed me photographs of faults made in the lace by the machines and I wondered how these could be repaired, but Alf assured me that they were. All I can say is these ladies must have been extremely deft of finger and with keen eyesight.

Ernie Ovey, whom I have previously mentioned, told me that his father, grandfather and uncles were all lace makers. His grandfather, John, worked until he was 76 years old and his father Fred went into the mill at the age of 14. Fred wanted to join the Army but his father wouldn't agree, so he ran away to Ilfracombe to catch a steamship to Wales, so he could work in the mines. His father was so perturbed by this idea that he went after Fred and

relented, allowing him to join the Army. Fred joined the Devonshire Regiment and was wounded at the Somme in the First World War, then returned to work at the lace factory. Ernie can clearly recall going to the factory as a child to take his father a jug of tea and watch him at work at the looms.

Mary Stribling, who was born in Princess Street, left school at 14 and joined her father and her sister Betty at the factory. Mary and Betty were bobbin winders. She told me that she loved her work at the factory, although it was hard. She worked 48 hours a week for £3.4s.

Chris Hammett left the Boys' Secondary Modern School at the age of 15 and went straight across the road to start work at the factory. He was a warper and once again, when explaining this work to me, I was in awe at how nimble the workers had to be, with delicate tasks such as unravelling knotted threads and rejoining broken ones so that they were not visible in the finished material.

Over almost two centuries the factory has had a chequered history that went along with the fragile fortunes of the world trade in cotton. However, since 1929 John C. Small & Tidmas have been the owners and although lace production was transferred to their other factories in Nottingham and South Chard in the 1970s they are still involved in the 'rag' trade at the Barnstaple site.

The industries I have covered so far are still in business and flourishing in one way or another, but the remaining trades are no longer in existence in Barnstaple.

Above: *Dr John Marston playing his harpsichord.*

Above: *John Marston with Alan Sowden, who helps him in his five acres of garden.*

Right: *Talented sculptress Vanessa Marston in her studio with one of her pieces of work, called 'Girl on a Swing'.*

ঙ Lace Making ঙ

Gorwell House, built by John Miller who owned the lace factory.

Below: *Allotments belonging to the lace factory, which were allocated to the workers.*

Above: *The curved railway bridge that took the trains from Barnstaple Junction to the Quay Station and later the Town Station.*

Right: *Cecil Gammon and Ricky Richards with one of the ploughs made at Huxtables.*

Left: *Workmen outside Huxtables Agricultural Engineers.* Left to right: *Leonard Harwood, ?, Les Bowen, Cecil Gammon, Bob Gunningham, Norman Pim, ?.*

Foundries

The Barnstaple Foundry stood at the bottom of Newport Road and in 1822 it was owned by Thomas Willshire and employed 50 men. Charles Willshire followed his father into the business until 1884 when Mr W.C. Rafarel became the proprietor. It was here that the pillars of the iron bridge that carried the famous curved railway line across the Taw were made, each weighing 25cwt. In its time this was easily the largest foundry in the town, making a wide range of ironmongery from agricultural implements to water-wheels, railings, church pillars, street-light pillars, gas- and waterworks castings and the railway lines from Barnstaple to Ilfracombe.

Thomas Lake, who had been an apprentice at the Barnstaple Foundry, joined his brother Edwin in his foundry at Victoria Street. Thomas built a second foundry in his back garden at 61 Newport Road. This became Thomas Lake and Son and continued until 1948 when it was sold to Huxtables Engineering.

John Huxtable, whose father, grandfather and great-grandfather were all confusingly called John, told me of his long family history of blacksmithing and founding. Great-grandfather, John Huxtable, who was born in 1820, was a blacksmith at Brayford. After his death in 1858 his son John took over the smithy at the age of 17, but did not stay as a blacksmith for long as he branched out into making farm implements, which he had the foresight to have patented. One of his first inventions was the 'turnover plough', which enabled the horse ploughman to go straight back across the field alongside the last furrow. He also made cultivators, chain harrows and hoes, all to his own design. In 1880 he invented the 'Trellis Rake' which flourished until 1960. Before this 'concertina' rake was designed farmers found it difficult to get wide rakes through gateways and along narrow lanes. In 1881 he moved to Filleigh where there was a water-wheel to drive the machinery in his workshop, but when several dry summers caused work to come to a standstill he moved to Barnstaple. The new premises were on the corner of Bear Street and Alexandra Road and became Huxtables Agricultural Engineers. John and his family of 12 children lived at Brayford House, Hills View. He carried on working until he died in 1919 when his son, also called John, took over. Not a robust man, he had to take early retirement. So, like his grandfather before him, the present-day John Huxtable had to take on the mantle of running the business at the age of 17, while still a student at Blundell's School. He told me that if it had not been for a splendid workforce of about 30 men to help him through his early years he would have found it very difficult, as not only did they have the engineering works but also an ironmonger's shop in Holland Street.

Huxtables worked closely with Thomas Lake's Foundry in Newport and eventually bought it. The foundry business soared but with the increase in production at Newport there were local complaints of the smoke and smell coming from the works. This led to a new foundry being built on Seven Brethren Bank in 1966. Later, Huxtables Agricultural Engineers was sold to Norringtons of Exeter and the foundry was sold to Brickhouse Dudley.

The Glove Industry

The story of Sanders Fellmongers and Pilton glove factory were closely entwined in their beginnings. In 1844 brothers Samuel and John Sanders purchased Bull Court at Pilton and turned the back of the building into a factory, producing rough agricultural gloves and gaiters. The firm employed 16 men in tanning and wool stapling. There seems to have been some family disagreement when Joseph Baylis joined the business 12 years later and John Sanders left the firm to farm at East Down. He later emigrated to New Zealand.

In 1869 Samuel also left the Pilton works to take over the premises belonging to the tanner James Rice on Pilton Causeway. This is where Sanders the fellmongers and the Pilton glove factory separate in history.

Joseph Baylis, who had previously worked for the glovers Dent, Allcroft & Co., developed the company to produce skins for high-fashion gloves for couture houses. In the following 20 years Baylis built a highly successful company employing over 200 staff within the factory, as well as home-workers. The gloves sold throughout the British Isles and Northern Europe – Norway, Sweden and Russia – and as far away as India, North America and Australia.

Shirley Sanders showed me a scrapbook of newspaper cuttings of the mayoral year of A.J. Reavell in 1907. From this I learned that Mr A.J. Reavell had married the niece of Joseph Baylis and in 1889 had taken over the running of the glove factory. As I have already mentioned, Mayor Reavell was a conscientious man who was a Congregationalist and was the Chairman of the North Devon Infirmary, as well as the Chairman of the Board of Secondary Education and Municipal Science and Art School. These newspaper cuttings also tell us that to celebrate their silver wedding anniversary and their son's wedding the Reavells took all the glove-factory workers on a day-trip to Lynton and Lynmouth on the railway.

Flossie Shapland, née Ingerson, was born in Pilton Street in 1907 and she told me of her father,

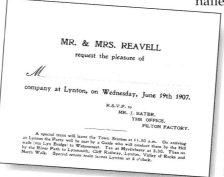

who worked at the factory all his life and for many years was the foreman. When she was three they moved to a worker's house at Lake Cottages and her mother put up net curtains at the kitchen window to shut out the 'nasty' view of the back of the factory. She recalls her father taking her to the factory field in Northfield Lane (now Nursery End housing estate) where she saw the skins being nailed up on frames to dry. Her father told her about 'scurfing' – scraping them to get the residue off the underside. This caused a cloud of dust, in which the men had to work.

For a short while Flossie's mother did outwork for the factory and Flossie remembers when she had to collect and return work for her. There was a window in the factory wall with boards over it. She had to knock on it and hand in the parcel of finished gloves, then wait for the new pile of work. The outwork was 'end tying' – tying and cutting the cotton ends of the three small darts on the back of the gloves.

Ellen Wallis, née Jenkins, lived at Prixford during the Second World War and in 1942 she went to work at the glove factory. She made silk lining for pilots' gloves. It was a vital piece of war work and on one occasion when she was too ill to go to the factory a sewing machine was taken to her home for her to complete her job.

Work at the factory started at 8a.m. and finished at 6p.m. Getting there was easy, as Prixford is two miles, mainly uphill from Pilton, so all she had to do was jump on her bike at 7.45a.m. and sail down the hills. Returning home after a tiring day at the sewing machine was a different matter, as she had to walk most of the way, pushing her bike. This was made worse one wet, dark night when she was told that a German fighter plane had crashed nearby and the pilot had escaped. She never did establish the whereabouts of the enemy but she certainly made it home in double quick time!

I do not know when the glove factory came under the ownership of Dents but it was always known by that name in my lifetime. Maureen Soby, née Jenkins, went to work at Dents in 1955. She had

An invitation to the workers of the glove factory for a day-outing to Lynton's railway to celebrate the silver wedding anniversary of Mr and Mrs Reavell.

Maureen Jenkins outside Dents glove factory in Pilton, 1957.

❧ Glove Making ❧

June Hutchings at her machine at the Newport factory, 1951.

Below: *Four friends on the steps of Dents glove-works in Newport, 1955. Pictured at the back is Phyllis Squires, with ? Behan in front with Sheila Hole and June Drayton (née Hutchings).*

Left: *Girls from the glove factory in the 1954 carnival.*
Photograph Knights Photographic.

Right: *Another carnival entry by the girls from Dents glove factory.*

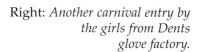

left the grammar school and worked in MacFisheries, but after four months of trying to get to like the smell of fish she handed in her notice. It was at Christmas time and her father was none too pleased with her rash action, so on the day after Boxing Day she was packed off to the Labour Exchange to find a job vacancy. By the end of the week she was the office junior at Dents glove factory and within nine months she was the export clerk.

Dents gloves were exclusive and prized articles of clothing when you had a special occasion to attend, according to Maureen. The leather and suede arrived at the factory already tanned and dyed. It would go to the cutting room where there were 20 cutters, then to the machine room, where there were about 50 women machinists, and then into the finishing room where two women pressed and smoothed the gloves over dummy hands. In the packing room the cellophane-wrapped gloves were placed in pale-green boxes. The gloves were sent all over the world and Maureen remembers six dozen white cotton gloves being sent to Ethiopia for the Imperial Guard. The Bahamian Police Force were also equipped with white cotton gloves all the way from Barnstaple. Christian Dior was another customer.

Dents had another small factory at the bottom of Newport, which mainly made fabric gloves. It was here that June Drayton, née Hutchings, started work in 1949 at the age of 15. Her first week's wages were 30s. which rose to between £5 and £6 when she was skilled. June enjoyed working at the Newport factory as, she said, it had a free and easy atmosphere. She also worked at the Dents glove factory at Pilton and a small glove factory in Reform Street, which did not belong to Dents. It was a very small factory, no bigger than a house, where only 12 to 14 women worked. Another happy memory for her is the carnival floats that the factory entered every year, nearly always winning first prize.

Fellmongering

We return now to the originators of the Pilton glove manufactory and Samuel Sanders, who moved his fellmongering business to Pilton Causeway in 1869. What is fellmongering? 'Fell' is the Saxon for skin and a 'monger' is a dealer. Most local people know this business as Sanders' sheepskin factory, which produced and sold rugs in a shop on the Causeway until 2001. Shirley Sanders, who is the wife of James – the great-grandson of Samuel – has researched the family history and has kindly allowed me to use it here.

The building on Pilton Causeway stood next to a leat and on the opposite side was the area known as Rackfield. Along the leat were tanneries and breweries which all needed a constant supply of water. The effluent from these manufactories emptied into the leat, which then flowed into the River Yeo. It was here that Samuel tanned the sheepskins.

To remove the wool from the skins they were soaked in pits of lime to loosen the wool, then placed on a sloping table where the wool was pulled off by hand, then graded and dried over coke fires. This was sold for clothing, wool or carpets. The pelts were used for boots or gloves.

The family continued fellmongering until 1972/73 when, due to problems such as the smell from the works affecting the houses that had grown up around the business, it was decided to discontinue the processing and concentrate on producing sheepskin rugs. Samuel also sold fertilizers to farmers and bought the wool that had been shorn from the sheep. Farmers settled their accounts once a year at the time of the Barnstaple Fair and it was the custom to set out long trestle-tables with whole hams and great joints of beef and barrels of cider to be enjoyed.

When Samuel's grandson Jim took over the business there was only a small shop selling sheepskin rugs

Samuel Sanders, the founder of Sanders and Son, in 1869.

Mill Leat, which ran between Rackfield and Sanders' sheepskin works.

Left: *Men working at the soak pits behind Rackfield, 1930.*

Below: *Loading wool from the Rolle Quay warehouse onto a Great Western Railway lorry.*

Right: *Dipping sheepskins in a vat.*

Left: *Andrew Withers combing a sheepskin.*

and slippers and the manufactory was still carried on in sheds outside. The business was enlarged when the Lynton railway was closed and Jim bought the adjacent engine sheds and land.

Many butchers had their own slaughtering facilities and sheepskins were collected by handcart. When Jim's son James joined the family business in 1953 he recalls that there were about 20 small

abattoirs in and around the town and it was his job to collect the skins from them.

James says the business was at its height in the 1960s and '70s when they had 35 to 40 men working for them and 25–30,000 skins were handled in a week. This family business closed in 2001 and at the time of writing there are plans to redevelop the site of this ancient trade.

Chapter Eight

BUTCHER, BAKER, CANDLESTICK MAKER...

This image: *Butcher's Row, c.1900.*
Below: *Samuel Ayre's shop in Joy Street, c.1925.*
Left to right: *Stanley Ayre, Harry Kent (the slaughterman), Wilma Ayre (Stanley's sister) and Samuel Ayre.*

I did not manage to find any candlestick makers to interview but did talk to several other tradesmen and women who have served the townsfolk of Barnstaple for many years. I will now share their memories of their working lives with you.

Butchers

Where better to start than with Ken Ayre, whose family were purveyors of meat and poultry in the town for four generations. Ken's grandfather, Samuel Ayre, learned his trade with Fred Elliott in his butcher's shop on the corner of the High Street and Holland Street and went on to open his own shop in Butcher's Row, then in 1920 bought bigger premises in Joy Street (the entrance to Banbury's at the time of writing). Samuel's son Stanley worked with him in the business and met his wife Ellie when she came to the butcher's by horse and trap to deliver pork from her parents' pig farm.

Ken, born in 1926, joined his father and grandfather in the butcher's shop when he was 14. He had actually been delivering meat on a cycle since

the age of nine. He says he was so small and the basket strapped to the front was so cumbersome that Archie Jones at the cycle shop made a pint-sized bike especially for him.

In 1947 Ken returned from service with the RAF and entered the family business on a weekly wage of £2.10s. a week. When his grandfather, Samuel, retired in 1951 Ken and his father, who Sam always fondly called 'the boys', took over the business. Ken recalls wartime rationing when every person was allowed 10d. worth of meat and 2d. worth of corned beef a week. Butchers had a permit for the number of customers registered with them and they had to collect the ration of meat from the Ice Factory in Rolle Street.

Above: *Samuel's wife, Ellie, delivering pork to the shop from their Goodleigh farm. Her sister-in-law Beat Ayre sits on the right of the horse and trap, 1920.*

Ken and his wife Stella outside the shop in the 1960s.

When the rationing finished Ken decided that they should go back to buying their own meat direct from the farmers as his grandfather had done. He also bred his own pigs at home. He had an old van in which he would travel around the farms to buy chickens, 200 at a time. His mother killed and dressed the birds for the shop.

Ken admits he was not too experienced when it came to buying anything other than pigs. One day he went to a farm and picked out 20 lambs by live weight and agreed to go back another day to collect them. When he went back they were weighed again and Ken was caught out because previously, before they had been weighed the first time, the lambs had been out all night in the rain and their fleeces were full of water. He said he paid for 'an awful lot of rainwater'.

Ken is a larger-than-life character and anyone who knows him will not be surprised at what triggered his retirement – an over zealous traffic warden. He was trying to book Ken for parking his two vans in a restricted area of Joy Street. Ken had already had several altercations with traffic wardens and this was the last straw, so in a 'fit of pique' he told the traffic warden that he'd had enough and they'd driven him to retire. Ken says that within half an hour a reporter arrived in the shop to ask if it was true. The following day the newspaper headlines read 'Butcher Fights Bureaucracy'.

Ken hung up his butcher's apron for the last time in 1976. However, his son Stuart carried on the family business with another butcher's shop that Ken had bought in Bear Street.

As mentioned, Fred Elliott had a shop which was on the corner of High Street with his house behind in what is, at the time of writing, Holland Walk. Fred followed his father into the butchering trade. His father also had a farm at Ashford. Michael James, whose family owned the greengrocers and florists on the opposite side of Holland Walk, remembers Fred as a kindly man who often wore a frock coat.

In 1934, at the age of 16, Iris Crook went to work as a house parlour-maid for Mrs Elliott who thought that the name Iris was too flowery for her position so called her by her middle name, Grace – a name that somehow stuck for 40 years. She was paid 5s. a week and lived in the Elliotts' house. Although she was employed to work in the house it was expected that, with the cook, she would scald the milk brought in by Mr Elliott senior from the farm twice a day. This would be turned into cream and butter and sold at the back door of the house. They also had to render down the lard in a big vat over a gas stove and put it in wax bags where it solidified and was sold in the butcher's shop. They made the brawn too.

Iris told me that she did not enjoy the work and left when she secured a job across the road at the Central Restaurant as a waitress, earning 12s. a week plus tips. This change of job was a happy one – it led to her meeting her future husband Arthur, when he came to the restaurant for a meal while on exercise with the Territorial Army.

Bakers

I visited Dick Raymond at his home on the edge of Exmoor where he told me of his family bakery business. His grandfather, Francis William Raymond, started the bakery in Maudlin Street and in 1893 moved to 81 Boutport Street. Dick showed me a scrap of paper on which his grandfather had written a notice to be put in the newspaper. It reads:

North Devon Journal Herald *July 13 1893.*
NOTICE OF REMOVAL
Frank Raymond Begs to inform his customers and the Public generally that in consequence of increasing Business he has removed from Maudlin Street to 81 Boutport Street where with extensive storage facilities he will in future be able to supply any quantities of Flour, Meal, Maize, Oats and Bran at prices startling, at the same time assuring his Patrons that the quality is incomparable.
Try Raymond's noted Home-Made Bread Supplied Daily as Before.

❧ *Bakers* ❧

Left *Horace Raymond with the shop's horse and bread van, c.1920.*

Below, left: *John Richards with one of his trophies for confectionery.*

Above: *Richards bakery staff preparing for a day-trip.*

Below: *John Richards in his bakehouse behind the shop at Mermaid Cross.*

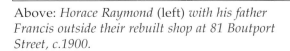

Above: *Horace Raymond (left) with his father Francis outside their rebuilt shop at 81 Boutport Street, c.1900.*

Frank and Rose Raymond had four children. Dick's father Horace was the eldest and later ran the bakery. The youngest son was Stanley who had a men's outfitters shop in the High Street.

Dick was born above the bakery in Boutport Street in 1924 and after leaving grammar school at 15 became a bread roundsman with a horse and cart. He didn't like this, so went to County Garage and worked on a 1914 Crossley fire engine instead! He was paid 5s. a week but 1d. was deducted for the Red Cross. Dick joined the wartime RAF and returned to the bakery in 1948 where he worked with his wife Rose until they retired in 1983.

The Raymonds had another shop in the High Street. As the bakery was behind the shop in Boutport Street, all the bread, cakes and pasties had to be carried on trays on the bakers' heads from Boutport Street and through the churchyard to the High Street. When Dick first took over there were only two run-down old machines and four members of staff. When they sold the business in 1983 there were 52 staff and they produced 100 dozen pasties by 8a.m.

Dick recalls a lovely old chap called Bill Cockle who would start work at 3a.m. One of the clapped-out machines was a dough mixer with belting that went up through the ceiling to a motor in the engine-room that sparked so much, Dick says, you could read a book by spark-light! On the occasions when the belting began to slip Bill had a tin of jam and a stick, he would flick the jam at the belt to get it to hold.

There were several other bakeries in the town and among the best remembered by local people are Bromley's, Pearce's and Richard's, which were all in the High Street.

Michael Bromley told me that in 1924 the family obtained the property at the rear of the High Street shop and built a ballroom and snack bar which opened out on to the Strand. On the side of this building was the bakery and it was here that the bread and pastries were made, as well as an extravaganza of cakes, especially wedding cakes. Bromley's will always be remembered for their excellent cakes, pastries and the waitresses in their black uniform dresses with frilly white aprons.

A few yards further up the street was Pearce's cake shop and tearooms which competed with Bromley's for its expertise in the confectionery arts. Peggy Huxtable told me that her grandfather, Thomas Pearce, was a baker in Newport whose son Ralph followed his father into the business and trained in Switzerland as an 'artist confectioner'. He later opened the shop and tearooms in the High Street. Norah Maynard from Atherington remembers when she was a little girl being taken by her mother on special occasions for tea and a plate of delicious fancy cakes to one of these well-known teashops; a memory no doubt shared by many of us.

John Richards served his bakery apprenticeship with Bromley's and in his early years worked as a pastry chef at the North Gate Hotel. He also swept the board with prizes and silver trophies for his excellence in confectionery. He was a much-liked man in the town and is remembered for his smile and rotund figure. Yvonne Webber, his niece, has memories of visiting her Uncle John in the flat above his shop where he lived at the North Gate end of the High Street. When Yvonne and her elder sister Sheila went there they would have to look smart and be on their best behaviour. Yvonne always felt she was being presented to the grandfather figure for his approval. He would take them downstairs to the bakehouse, where they were allowed to choose a fancy from the stacked trays of cakes.

Once a year John Richards took his staff and their families on a day out. Yvonne recalls trays full of pasties, pies and cakes appearing when it was lunch-time.

Milk delivery around Barnstaple, c.1920.

Captain on his milk round at Yeo Vale.

Abby Drew is pictured on the right of the group outside Pow's Dairy in Castle Street.

*Lionel Weston delivering milk in
Barbican Terrace in 1950.*

Milkmen

As mentioned previously, Abby Drew lived for many years in Azes Lane and at the age of just seven he did a milk round. On leaving school he worked full time for Pow's Dairy in Castle Street. Abby made two deliveries every day with fresh or scalded milk and cream (fresh milk was straight from the cow and scalded milk was what was left over after the farmer's wife had warmed it and removed the cream to sell separately). He later went on to own the business for 20 years.

One of his memories is of the fair week when he delivered to the caravans belonging to the fair folk. Mr Pow bought a handcart and Abby would take two churns of milk and baskets of butter, eggs and cream. He told me of the time he called at a caravan which had a cupboard outside where the order and money were left. On this occasion they were not there so he knocked on the door. Abby was pop-eyed when the man who answered the door went to a tea chest, which was bursting with 3d. and 6d. pieces. The money was obviously the takings from the fair rides.

Arthur Squires related the story of when his father worked for the Albion Dairy in Green Lane.

Hubert Watts at Fatstock Show.

He did his round with a pony and float. One Sunday in Pilton Street he told his young novice assistant that the lady in the house opposite wanted half a pint of milk. Arthur explained that:

This old lady was stone deaf and had a hearing aid, the trumpet kind. The old dear saw the young man coming up to the door and pushed out her ear-trumpet, which he promptly filled with her half pint!

Next we come to a milk lady who also started work straight from school at the age of 14. Sheila Edwards, née Snow, lived in Gloster Road, Newport and worked at first for Mr Watts, who had a dairy in their street. She rode a tricycle with a metal basket on the front to hold the milk churns from which she ladled the milk into customers' jugs. She only worked until lunch-time so when the war started in 1939 Mr Wallis, the newsagent in Church Lane, asked her to take on the delivery of newspapers to Gloster Road, which she did in the afternoon. Then when she was 16 Sheila went to work full time for Mrs Waldron at the Newport Dairy (the thatched house opposite Victoria Street), delivering the milk around the Newport area. Mrs Waldron asked Sheila if she would learn to drive, so before long she was doing her round in a Morris 8. She had a wooden box with a large churn in the back of the car. She would stop in the street and housewives would come out to her with their jugs. In the afternoons she cycled to the Waldrons' farm at Bishops Tawton, clean out the dairy and wash out the quarter-pint bottles for the next day's milk for the primary school next door. In the summer, after tea at the farm, she would either carry hay at Newbridge or stack corn at Codden Hill. In September there was potato picking and sugar beet to be lifted at Chestwood. A railway wagon would be delivered to the field and they had three days to fill it before it was taken back to the G.W. Station at Victoria Road for transportation.

Sheila especially recalls the bad winter of 1947 and the deep snow, when she had to put chains on the wheels of the car so she could deliver the milk and had to walk to Bishops Tawton in the afternoons.

There was another Watts Dairy in the town, in Boutport Street. Roger Watts told me of his grandfather Henry who started the business in 1896. He kept 20 milking cows at Underwood Meadows at Raleigh, from where the milk was taken to the dairy and then sold around the town twice a day. Horse-drawn floats delivered the milk until 1962 when electric ones replaced them.

Henry died in 1929 and his son Hubert carried on the farming and dairy business with his mother. In 1953 Hubert purchased Pitt Farm in Raleigh and the family moved there. Eight people worked in the dairy and on the farm. Roger joined the family business in 1961 and remembers Bill Turner who lived in Yeo Vale and could turn his hand to any job on the farm and deliver the milk around the streets. Similarly, Lionel Weston and his wife Yvonne also worked on the farm. The business was sold to Express Dairies in 1973 when Hubert retired.

I went to visit the Westons at their home at Raleigh Cottages where Lionel told me his memories of his time with the dairy. He had been working for Hubert and Alice Watts on a milk round before school each morning since the age of 11. He would deliver seven gallons of milk each morning by bicycle and when he got back to the farm Mrs Watts had breakfast ready for him; eggs and bacon on a plate, or if he was late, made into a sandwich. When Lionel left school at 14 he went to work full time at the dairy. He had been offered a job at Central Garages at 12s.6d. a week, but his Dad had just died so he took the job at the dairy as that paid 15s. a week. He worked on the farm and on a twice-daily milk round for the next 32 years.

Lionel recalled his horse, Prince, who he said was 'the brainiest horse you ever knowed'. He told me of the day he left Prince outside a 'certain property' in Boutport Street (i.e. the Horse and Groom pub) and the horse got fed up with waiting so made his way home to the farm over a mile away and stood outside the dairy. Lionel has high praise for Hubert Watts and says that:

He was a good Christian gentleman who treated everyone with respect. He would never ask anyone to do anything he was not prepared to do himself. If he asked me to be at work at 6 o'clock in the morning he'd cycle up past our cottage at ten to six and be there before me.

Another lady farmer with a milk round, who I am assured had an eye to business, was Ruby Jackman. Her daughter Monica Wonnacott told me how hard her parents worked when she was young. They had very little money after moving to their first farm near Cobbaton. Monica remembers her mother going out into the fields and picking parsley and whatever the last tenant farmer had left. Then, after filling empty Corona lemonade bottles with milk she loaded up a horse and trap and went into Barnstaple, knocking on doors until she had sold her goods. She later had a Sunbeam car and Monica recalls tying baskets of strawberries to the running-boards to sell around the streets. Ruby was not known for her prowess with the automobile and the story goes that when she was seen approaching everyone would dive for the hedge! Mondays would be spent in the kitchen making hogs puddings and chitterlings for sale on the round. Monica says her mother was a bit of a Robin Hood character as she remembers one Christmas when Ruby did a poultry draw and, after reading the name on the winning ticket, said, 'Oh they don't need this turkey because they've got plenty of money. Let's give it to Mrs X who has six kiddies and no money.'

Ruby sold everything from milk, cream and butter to vegetables, fruit, eggs and meat. She would always try to be first on the round before Jimmy Vellacott the vegetable man got there. Some of her customers were not very helpful, like the lady who would come out to the van and say, 'Now Mrs Jackman, what shall I have today? Cissy doesn't like cauliflower and Reg don't like cabbage.' She would then recite all her six children's likes and dislikes and finally announce, 'Aw give us a penath of scald today.' And this would go on day after day; not helpful when you have a large round to complete.

During the war Ruby took on the 'Men from the Ministry'. Milk rounds were zoned in the town, which meant that the farmers who came into town to sell their milk were likely to lose their livelihood. Ruby fought this tooth and nail and after many months won her case. Life was also made difficult as by now they had two dairies and at times the Land Army girls would have to work up to 18 hours a day to get through all the milk preparation. Fuel was in short supply and Monica recalls that they not only had to push-start the vans and free-wheel down hills but quite often they had to push them up the other side!

In the early 1940s Monica's parents bought 3 High Street to use as a dairy, but afterwards the Americans commandeered the building. As Ruby

Mrs Ruby Jackman.

could not use the High Street shop she bought a dairy at Sticklepath. While she was waiting for health regulation work to be completed on the drains she found there was more money to be made selling food as a café, so she sold her milk rounds. The story of Jackman's Café is continued in Chapter Ten.

Drapers

Whenever I ask people about their memories of Lake's the drapers in Boutport Street, the answer is 'We remember the railway on the ceiling.' After a purchase the shop assistant would put the customer's money and invoice into a small wooden box which was attached to a pulley. When it was tugged it sent the box hurtling at what seemed a phenomenal speed along wires on the ceiling to the cashier in her office upstairs. The change and receipt would return by the same system. I remember as a little girl sitting on the high stools beside the glass counters watching in wonderment at this whole procedure. I loved to wander around the shop with its assortment of materials, embroidery silks, multi-coloured wools and shelves of small box drawers containing every article of haberdashery any seam-stress could want. As my mother was a talented dressmaker who made all her own and my clothes our visits to the emporium were very frequent.

Mabel Bray, a Cornish girl from Camelford, moved to Barnstaple with her sister Emily to work and live-in as draper's assistant at Mr Catford's shop at 104 Boutport Street. In 1904 she married Charles Lake, the son of Thomas Lake who owned the foundry at Newport, and in 1905 they took over Catford's drapery business. Their son Leonard wrote that his mother's life was almost completely wrapped up in the business. She had little taste for domestic matters but ample ability to see they were adequately organised. She was a brilliant buyer and, with no training except experience and no form of stock control other than an unusual memory, the enterprise flourished. Leonard wrote that they took over a narrow but deep building with a stockroom, dining-room and kitchen at the rear and three bedrooms upstairs. There were bare plank floors and no showroom or fitting room. The whole place was lit most dangerously by open gas burners. The staff consisted of Mabel, her sisters Emily and Vera and an errand boy, William Cox. Charles Lake did the accounts alongside his 72-hour week at the foundry. The weekly wage bill during the first year was 22s.6d. The hours of business were between 8a.m. and 8p.m. but on Fridays they remained open until 9p.m. and on Saturdays never closed before 11p.m.

At the end of the first year of trading and after the heart-searching decision on the frivolous purchase of a piano for £10 the accounts showed a healthy surplus of £350. In 1906, Mabel's sister Vera returned to Camelford, a new assistant was taken on and a maid was employed for the household. She was paid 5s. a week plus keep. In 1907 electric lighting was made available so the Lakes gave up gas lighting and added their first modern amenity. In 1908 Leonard was born and Vera promptly returned to act as his nurse.

Sam White, who ran a business as a shoemaker, newsagent and shipping agent, occupied the property between Lake's drapers and the Corner House public house. In 1910 he retired and the Lakes took over the premises which provided space for a much-needed showroom and window display. Upstairs were three additional bedrooms, which meant the family and

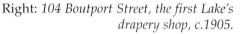

Right: *104 Boutport Street, the first Lake's drapery shop, c.1905.*

Left: *Lake's extended premises including the shipping agency, c.1910.*

83

❧ Drapers ❧

Right: *The Corner House public house on the corner of Joy Street before it was rebuilt in 1934.*

Below: *Margaret Lock ('Lockie') and Joy Brown (née Parsley) taking a break on the roof of Horace Mann's shop in 1939.*

Above: *Builders working on the 18-month project of rebuilding the Corner House, one half at a time.*

Above: *Horace Mann's staff at their closing-down party at the Three Bears Café, 1959.*
Left to right, back row: ?, Scoins, ?, Ellicott, Robinson;
centre: Kerry, Pugsley, Lidstone, Roberts, Johns, Cook;
seated: Stone, Beer, Parsley, Kivell, Harvey, Pugsley and Crang.
(Only surnames were supplied with this photo).

live-in staff could make themselves more comfortable. It was decided to retain the shipping agency and Charles largely ceased his foundry work and concentrated on this side of the business. The agency proved profitable, as work in North Devon was not very plentiful and agricultural labourers were in great demand in Australia and Canada. Assisted passages cost only £2 or £3 and large numbers of workers emigrated.

During the First World War Mabel excelled with her business acumen and she maintained a healthy profit for the shop. The foundry at Newport came under increasing demand and Charles had to become involved with its activities again. In March 1916 Mabel and Charles had the opportunity to purchase their business properties from the Clinton estates. The price was £1,785.10s., which they thought reasonable. Imagine their surprise and delight when they discovered on completion that they had also become the owners of the Corner House! The site covered a total of 9,000 square feet and the Corner House was let to brewers Arnold and Hancock. When Leonard left school in 1924 he joined the family business, although he agrees that his attendance was rather spasmodic and he did spend a great deal of time on the golf course and with his motorsport. Perhaps it was his interest in cars that led him to work at County Garage as a salesman in 1927. However, he was soon persuaded that there was more profit to be made in the drapery trade so he rejoined the firm in 1928. In 1931 he became an equal partner with his parents and also a marriage partner to Betty Stanbury, granddaughter of Richard Stanbury who owned the flour mill on Rolle Quay.

The arrival of the Marks and Spencer store in 1934 hit Lake's in the profit margin, but this was overcome by the next year. It was also in this year that the brewer's lease on the Corner House ran out and the Lakes decided to rebuild the premises, which can be seen in 2002 as the public house and two lock-up shops joining the Royal Exchange in Joy Street. Rebuilding took 18 months and involved moving the whole building back by 6 feet to widen the street. For this the Town Council paid £700. Charles took over the running of this new hostelry and Thomas Garland was employed as the manager. Tommy Garland was a young man, recently married, whose only experience of the licensed trade was a six-month period as steward at the Barnstaple and District Club. However, he became a very much-liked and respected licensee over many years.

Mabel's stock-buying excelled once again during the Second World War, with many evacuated women and children in the local area needing clothing and a big demand for blackout material, all of which Lake's could provide due to her business foresight. Mabel died in 1953 at the age of 78 and Charles died in 1957. Leonard wrote of his mother that due to her restricted upbringing she had a fear of taking business risks (that seems hard to believe!).

But she was unarguably a great draper and buyer and, although she was sometimes tough and difficult, she was loved and respected by everyone who worked with or for her. My thanks to Leonard's daughter, Elizabeth Isaac, for allowing me to use her father's family history.

Joy Browne left school in 1939 and started work in the millinery department of the ladies' outfitters, Horace Mann. Everyone was known by their surname and Christian names were never used. The uniforms were all black – dress, stockings, shoes – and no make-up could be worn. The shop's errand-boy was named Kivell. Boy? He was in his 50s! He delivered customers' hats in a wooden hatbox on his bike.

At 18 Joy went to Westlands aircraft factory at Yeovil to do war work. At 21 she returned to Barnstaple to live at Prospect Cottages, Newport and went back to work at Horace Mann's, where she stayed until the business closed six months after Mr Mann died in 1959.

Horace Mann told Joy that he learnt his trade in London and his father gave him £100 to start his own business. He leased his first shop at 93a High Street where he sold household linen. He would display lots of haberdashery on the pavement outside the shop and he later leased the front of the shop next door. In this window he would display sheets and blankets. Mr Mann then expanded upstairs with a coat department with a few suits and coats. He had an agreement with his supplier on a 'sale or return' basis, just in case the line of business did not take off. Joy explained that Horace Mann was very religious and a perfect gentleman to his staff, although a stickler for perfect 'business behaviour'. On occasions customers took advantage of his good nature. In the millinery department they had a policy that customers could have anything on approval for a week. Joy said that at this time hats were worn for all occasions – weddings, funerals, christenings and anniversary Sundays. It was not unknown for a hat to be taken on approval on a Friday and brought back the following week after its first outing on the Saturday! When a hat was returned Miss Hillier (Hilly) inspected the band inside and if it was greasy she would replace it and put the hat back on display.

Hilly was the shop's milliner who could make fantastic creations or remake and restore old hats. She had a metal hat block and ladies would bring in their hats to be re-blocked and cleaned. This meant heating the block and steaming it. On one occasion a lady brought in an ivory straw hat she wanted remodelled. It was a Friday morning and they were very busy so Hilly had to help out on the shop floor. She left the hat on the block and when she returned the straw had turned a deep shade of biscuit. However, with a little 'tweaking' and the help of biscuit-coloured ribbon the customer was quite happy with her 'new' creation.

The shop would alter anything purchased there for over £5 without charge. So you can imagine there was a large workroom, which housed nine staff. Joy recalls one lady who was over 6 feet tall and they made two identical coats into one for her, which of course meant completely taking them apart and remaking them for free.

Horace Mann's always did a good trade in funeral clothing and Joy, who was in charge of the coat and dress department, recalls that they had a large stock of black coats which had been on the rail for so long they had to be continually brushed and sprayed for moths. After Horace Mann died the business was wound up, which meant having to get rid of all the stock. The black coats were a problem until an executor of his will suggested that Joy put them in the window with a price tag of £1 each. They were all sold by lunch-time!

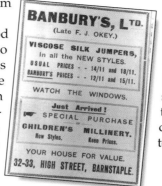

A newspaper advertisement from 1925.

Returning to errand boys, it became apparent to me when interviewing people that many boys worked in between school hours delivering goods around the town for traders. Lads such as George Laity and George Hewitt worked for Smyths, the ladies' dress shop in the High Street opposite Butcher's Row. George Laity told me that because the errand boys were not insured to use the shop's delivery bike they had to walk everywhere. There were few delivery vans until after the Second World War and most of the town deliveries were made on foot or by carrier bicycle.

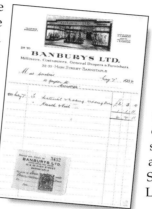

A Banbury's receipt.

Banbury's is the only one of the drapers and outfitters I have mentioned that still remains at the time of writing. I met Robert and David Banbury in their office at their Barnstaple High Street shop where they told me some of the history of their family business.

Arthur Stanley Banbury established Banbury's Ltd, Drapers and Furnishers, in Barnstaple in 1925. He had been a travelling salesman in East Anglia and was an astute businessman who travelled around by train with between six and eight trunks full of his merchandise. When he arrived at the designated station he would pay a porter to transport his trunks to his first client. If the shop owner/potential customer said he was too busy to see him, Arthur had a trick of producing small bargains from his pocket to whet the appetite and imagination. Attention caught, he would get the railway porter to bring in the rest of his paraphernalia.

One customer, Mr Horwood in Colchester, told Arthur of a drapers shop he knew of which was for sale in Barnstaple. With Mr Horwood's help and another silent partner backing him Arthur Banbury purchased the High Street store. In later years Mr Horwood's son, J.B. Horwood, came to the store as the assistant managing director.

At this time people paid their accounts yearly, usually on fair Friday when everyone from town and country came to Barnstaple. Like many of the town businesses Arthur entertained his customers to lunch (after they had settled their accounts) in his restaurant above the shop overlooking the High Street. The next day he would go to London on the train to pay his own yearly dues to his silent backer. He took the money in cash and so that he did not lose it or have it stolen his wife Gwendolyn sewed it into his pockets. Much amusement was created when he arrived and had to unstitch his pockets to retrieve the money.

Arthur Banbury was an extremely well turned-out and dapper dresser and always wore a fresh

Arthur Banbury.

The High Street with Banbury's shop on the right, c.1930.

Peter Banbury.

buttonhole in his jacket every day. Robert Banbury remembers his grandmother taking him to pick an early morning rose from their garden for his grand-father's buttonhole. Another daily ritual was to go into the barbers in Joy Street for a shave before the start of his working day.

When young ladies came in to choose a wedding dress he had a special joke for them. It went something like this:

I know what you'll be thinking of on your wedding day. When you go into the church you will think of walking up the aisle. And at the top of the aisle you'll see the altar. You'll look around and see the board with the hymns you will sing during the wedding service and you will think: I'll alter him!

This play on words – aisle, altar, hymn – was always a winner.

Arthur and Gwendolyn had one son, Peter, who was a keen rugby player with the Barnstaple Chiefs. He married Pamela and had four children – Robert, David and twins Richard and Jenny. In 1970 Peter died, leaving Robert aged 20 and David aged 18 to take over and run the business, which they have done most successfully, but both say it could not have been done without tremendous support from staff and family.

One last story from Robert is about a lady who purchased a suitcase and returned to complain that she couldn't release the strap. This was secured with 'Velcro' but she complained that she was having trouble undoing the 'Viagra'!

At the time of writing, Banbury's has not only extended in ground-floor size but also owns a furnishing department in Boutport Street, a sister store at Tiverton, a large warehouse on the outskirts of Barnstaple and the garden centre at Ashford.

Grocers

Woollacotts Grocers of 42 Bear Street, c.1910.

Abby Drew informed me that when he was a young lad there were as many as ten grocery shops in the High Street. From the Square end these included the Maypole, the Home and Colonial opposite the *North Devon Journal* offices, Dunns (where Somerfield is in 2002), Prideaux opposite Cross Street, Pearks on the corner of Joy Street, the Co-op, Ridds (who also had a grocery at the top of Azes Lane), Lipton and Ashton's.

This brings me to my chat with Sheila Gear whose mother, Winnie Ashton, was the youngest of five children born to Lawrence and Polly Ashton, who lived over their shop on the corner of Gammon Lane. Sheila remembers her granny Polly saying, 'Would you like a bar of chocolate my dear?' Sheila replied, 'I don't mind, Grandma,' and was reprimanded; 'You either say yes please, or no thank you.' Something Sheila has never forgotten. Sheila's daughter Glenda Tucker has a similar memory of Polly's eldest son William, who took over the family business after his mother died. He asked Glenda if she would like a biscuit, to which she replied, 'I don't know,' and was told 'You don't get one, then, because you either want one or you don't want one.' Old habits die hard!

Lawrence Ashton was a well-known and respected businessman who was also the Master of the Barnstaple Staghounds. He died aged 62 in 1915 when his youngest daughter Winnie was only 16 years old. His wife Polly carried on the business. During the First World War, when both sons were away at the Front, Winnie was the first woman to ride a motorcycle in Barnstaple *(see photo below)*.

Winnie Ashton (later Becklake) who rode this motorcycle around the town to collect orders from their customers, 1916.

Below: *Staff members outside Ashton's grocery shop on the corner of High Street and Gammon Lane, c.1900.*

Right: *Polly Ashton who, with her husband Lawrence, ran Ashton's grocers. Lawrence died in 1915 and Polly carried on the business with the help of her son William.*

She would visit their customers on her motorbike and deliver their orders by horse and trap.

Ford and Lock in Boutport Street was a grocery shop which stirred the senses of sight and smell. Diane Bosence was a cashier and she told me it was well known for its ground coffee – 'the smell was delicious.' Diane remembers how their clientele appreciated the personal service. They would sit on a wooden stool at the counter while butter was cut and patted into decorative shapes and sugar and other dry commodities were weighed and packed by assistants Jock Miller and Jack Norman in thick blue paper bags. Children would be given a biscuit from a jar kept on the counter. If a customer did not have a monthly account the shop assistants made out an invoice to take across to the cashier and pay for their purchases.

Dorothy Garman worked in the back of the shop doing up the orders and her husband Walter delivered them around the town on his bike, as well as working in the shop. Bill Chugg drove the van and delivered the orders outside the town.

The International Stores was another shop where I remember as a child sitting at the highly polished wooden counters whilst my mother and grandmother ordered their groceries. The aroma of freshly cured bacon and ground coffee comes flooding back to me. Also the sawdust on the scrubbed floor, which would crunch underfoot, and the bright white of the full-length starched aprons the assistants wore. Even as a young child I was aware of the individual attention and politeness every customer received.

Greengrocers

The family histories of two of Barnstaple's greengrocery businesses have been shared with me. Still going strong at the time of writing is Smallridge's in Holland Walk, run by Tony James, the grandson of the original owners Frank and Winifred James. Their son Michael told me about his memories of his working life. His family came to live in Barnstaple in 1938 from their original home in Kingsbridge and their first shop was at 71 High Street, on the corner of Holland Walk. They later opened a second shop at the lower end of Boutport Street. Mike's first job was also his last job! He went into the family business at the age of 15 and stayed there for the next 45 years. He started with the usual job of errand boy and delivered to the gentry of the town. He had to deliver to the back door of these houses where the staff were always dressed in uniforms. The firm bought fresh produce from Lady Fortescue's garden at Filleigh and in the spring he used to go to Saunton Court, the home of Lady Whitesmith, to pick daffodils to sell in the shop.

Mike was known as the shop's florist and when I asked him who taught him the art he recalled Hedley Exell, who was employed as their florist and was years in advance of his time with floral decoration. Mike made the Queen's bouquet from local blooms when she came to Barnstaple in 1956.

Busiest times of the year were the strawberry season and Christmas and as Mike was responsible for the majority of wedding bouquets he had to work over Easter, Christmas and weekends. A funeral order meant working all night to get the wreaths prepared. Mike also recalled that when he delivered the wreaths, especially out in the countryside, he would be expected to go into the parlour to pay his respects to the deceased.

Mike's wife Jean, who also worked in the shop with many of the other family members, said that at times Mike worked round the clock. They ordered flowers by phone from Covent Garden at night, which were put on the train at London the next morning and arrived in Barnstaple at 5p.m. If the porters didn't take them off the train at Exeter they would go on to Penzance! Mike says the quality of flowers today is far superior. Now they come by refrigerated van straight from the growers in Holland. He recalls collecting moss from Exmoor – it is now an offence to do this – today it is cultivated and delivered in a box. Once every flower had to be wired. Now they are placed in oasis pads. The Smallridge floristry imprint continues in the town as Mike's nephew, Tony James, has been very involved in the success of the annual Britain in Bloom competition.

Clarice Gee and her twin sister Betty told me about their mother Clara, who had a greengrocery and flower shop at 4 Litchdon Street from 1922. Their father, William Gee, had been badly affected by gas in the First World War. The shop had been a butcher's where William worked, but the butcher had money difficulties so William borrowed money from Clara to help him out. That's when Clara got involved as she said, 'If my money is going over there I'm going as well to see what happens to it.' She started by introducing fruit, vegetables and tinned foods. She was the first person to display a hand of bananas in her shop window! Fred Knill imported them into Barnstaple and Clara had the first ones. She later displayed a large vase of flowers in the window as decoration and before long someone asked if they were for sale. She sold those, put two more in the window and so her florist trade began.

When they were older Clarice and Betty helped their mother with a stall in the market on Fridays. Before school started they would push a handcart loaded with fruit and flowers to the market and set out the stall. After school they helped to collect everything together and take it back to the shop. They had the stall for more than 30 years. Clara died in 1980 at the age of 93.

✺§ Greengrocers §✺

Right: *Mrs James outside her greengrocery in the High Street. Note the appearance of Holland Walk before it was given a facelift.*

Left: *Smallridge's floral float in the 1954 carnival.*

Right: *The Flower Show in the Pannier Market in the 1950s. Left to right: Hedley Excell, Mike James and his father Frank.*

Left: *Clara Gee outside her shop in Litchdon Street.*

Below: *View of the Pannier Market from the High Street, 1932. Clarice Gee is the girl looking towards the camera on the front left of the picture. Her mother had a stall here for 30 years.*

The Pannier Market: Past & Present

A composed photograph by R.L. Knight of women selling from their panniers.

Below: *Doreen Fraser-Smith and Eileen White, both from Burrington, are pictured on the WI market stall.*

Above: *A postcard of the Pannier Market, c.1920.*

Right: *Chris Scott, who has been trading in the market for 60 years and used to come to market with her granny, selling her homemade jams and preserves with the help of her daughter Angela Shambrook.*

❧ The Pannier Market: Past & Present ❧

Right: *June Hemming showing a leg!*

Left: *Pat Rook selling flowers on Wyborn Brothers' stall at the entrance to the market in High Street.*

Right: *Tony Reynolds on his Westcountry Farm Cheese stall.*

Above: *Celia Fiennes from Stoke Rivers with her Mediterranean foods stall.*

Left: *An empty stall at the end of a long day. Marilyn Pine, who makes all her cakes at home, can be seen here with her mother, Margaret Worth, who helps her on market days.*

Right: *Cliff Bell with his holly garlands at the Christmas Market, 2000.*

Left: *Richard Shapland on his fruit and veg. stall with his children Jonathan and Laura, who were enjoying the Christmas Market atmosphere in 2000.*

Ironmongers

Stuart Slee worked in his father's ironmongery shop in Boutport Street (this is now Banbury's, next to the Queen's Hall). His father, Ernest, had started the business in the late 1920s. Stuart said that in the early days his father would travel around Exmoor on an old motorbike, calling on blacksmiths and village shops, carpenters and undertakers. The orders would then be delivered by a car and trailer or by a local carrier.

Ernest told Stuart that in those days people from Exmoor would only come to town once a year – at the time of the fair, when they would pay their bills and be given a meal before going to the fair. He also said that if they did not have the goods the customer wanted he would have to jump on his bike and dash round to the other ironmongers in the town and borrow it!

Stuart helped on Saturdays while still at school, then from the age of 14 he worked there full time. He recalls going around the villages in an old Standard 8 delivering goods, carrying out repairs and also installing Rayburns and Agas and removing the old Bodleys. Ernie Shobrook, a mason, helped him with these jobs. They also installed bottled-gas lighting to replace gas lamps. They sold tiled fire surrounds and Stuart delivered them in Barnstaple on a handcart because places like Derby and Queen Street were too narrow to get a van through. Stuart said that in Derby you would never find a door locked and were always invited to have a cup of tea. If no one was in you'd deliver your goods, pick up the money which was left on the table and shut the door on the way out. Sometimes there was a note which said 'Make yourself a cup of tea

Alfred and Ernest Slee outside their ironmongers shop in Boutport Street, c.1928.

and the buns are in the cupboard.' Stuart says it was a shame that when they pulled down all these old areas the people were rehoused in different parts of the town instead of keeping neighbours together. He also said the Derby people always paid their accounts promptly.

The store opened at 7a.m. and he had to wash the front of the shop and the pavement, then put all the wares on the ground outside. Goods were hung on hooks outside the windows as well. At 5p.m. all this had to be taken in and the floors cleaned. The furniture was cleared away and a sawdust and oil mix was spread over the floor then swept away, taking the dirt with it and leaving the pungent smell of oil.

Because they dealt with coffin furniture such as brass handles, brackets and name-plates, they were called on at all hours to supply these goods. In Slee's workshop at the back of the shop they kept such things as horseshoes, iron bars and paraffin. They also sold creosote and Stuart remembers one old gent who, when suffering from a cold, would come in and bend over the tank, taking a deep breath of the fumes to 'clear his head'.

Stuart says the end of the ironmongery trade came when multiple stores started to stock everything. For example, when Slee's sold a fireplace they would also sell the companion set that went with it, but then furniture shops started to stock them. They sold wax polishes, then Woolworth's and other shops began to. The Council used to deal with the four ironmongers in the town, but when the builders merchants started they lost this trade. Then the builders started buying their goods from far and wide and the local traders had one more nail in their coffins.

Right: H.R. Williams & Co. at 100 High Street in 1900.

Inside the Aladdin's Cave of Williams' Ironmongers, 1900.

Below: In 1900 H.R. Williams moved across the High Street to No. 10. This was later sold to become the Midland

Bank and Williams' moved back across the road to No. 100.

Talking of nails, Stuart reminded me of their shop where there were little drawers from floor to ceiling containing nails, screws, bolts, washers and the like. In those days there was no polythene or fancy plastic so when you bought saucepans or a dinner service they would be wrapped in brown paper to be carried home.

Other ironmongers in the town were Mortimer's in Boutport Street (which is now a sports shop), H.R. Williams (which is now a bookmakers), James and Tucker's shop (which was also in the High Street and is now a stationery shop) and Huxtables on the corner of Holland Street and Tuly Street.

John Shaddick's first job on leaving school was as an errand boy for James and Tucker. One of his tasks was to deliver goods on his carrier bike as far as Swimbridge, Braunton and Goodleigh, sometimes carrying as much as ten gallons of paraffin in cans. He also worked at Squires Agricultural Engineers in Tuly Street, opposite the slaughterhouse (which is the library at the time of writing). He recalls that a bullock escaped from the slaughterhouse and ended up in Huxtables shop, where it ran amok and lent an air of reality to the saying 'a bull in a china shop'!

Jewellers

We all probably have memories of our favourite jewellers in the town. For me it was Garnish and Winkles. Maybe it is all in the name, or perhaps because this is where I went with my husband-to-be to choose my wedding ring. Or maybe it was the shop itself which always had an old-world charm as you stepped down into it from the pavement in the High Street. Glass cases glittered with rings, necklaces and brooches and clocks ticked in unison round the walls. It was a cross between a scene from a Dickens novel and *Alice in Wonderland*.

James Winkles moved to Barnstaple from Birmingham in 1917 to work for Dark and Son in the High Street. The watch and clock repairer there was Lionel Garnish and in 1925 the two men set up in business together. James Winkles was a jeweller for 51 years and an authority on antiques, especially

Michael Hill at his workbench in 2001.

silver. When he died his son Kenneth took over the business and, with the help of his wife Mary, the shop remained until they retired in 1988.

Michael Hill, who is the fourth generation in his family's jewellery business, spoke to me at his shop in Joy Street. His great-grandfather, Benjamin Hill, established his Joy Street jewellery business in 1868. Michael reckons his is probably the oldest shop trading as the same family business in the town. Benjamin had five sons and two daughters. The five sons all worked in the jewellers until one left and became a jeweller in Hatherleigh, another went to Swansea and another died in 1904. The two daughters ran a fruit and vegetable business where Michael's shop is at the time of writing.

Benjamin died in 1901 and was buried at Bear Street cemetery. His gravestone reads simply:

BENJAMIN HILL
WATCHMAKER OF THIS TOWN.

Some time after the sisters retired the two shops once again became one and George Hill (Michael's grandfather) ran it until he died in 1932 at the age of 74. George had two sons, Roy and Peter. Roy (Michael's father) was only 19 years old when his father died and he took over the family business. In 1935 Peter joined the firm as the watch- and clockmaker. During the wartime, whilst Roy and Peter were in the Armed Services, watchmaker Frank Ridd helped Dora Hill, their mother, to carry on the business. In 1974 Michael joined the business but ran his own jewellers separately at 1 Joy Street as 'Facets', while his father and uncle carried on next door until 1985 when they retired and it was sold to Petre Glass.

Amusing anecdotes that Michael told me of his life in the shop included one about a gentleman of military bearing who walked in and demanded a table for two. Michael looked around his shop, which is very small (no more that 10 feet square) and said 'Sorry sir, this is a jewellers, not a café.' The military gentleman said, 'Gosh, you must think I'm mad,' did an about-turn and disappeared down the street. Another time a man walked in and said, 'I'm not buying anything. I just want to change my socks.' He sat down, took one shoe and sock off, then the other, swopped the socks and put on his shoes again, said, 'Thank you' and left without any explanation.

The final story has a touch of black humour. An elderly lady came into the shop and said, 'My husband came in two weeks ago and you fitted a new battery into his watch.' She then produced the watch. 'He died last week' she said, 'so I want you to take it out and give me the £2 back'!

Bicycle & Pram Shops

One morning, whilst sitting amongst rows of bicycles waiting for repair in John Webber's cycle and pram

Above: *Michael Bond repairing a cycle at Cyril Webber's Cycle Shop in Bear Street.*

Left: *Joan and Cyril Webber when they were members of the Barnstaple Imperial Wheelers Club in 1940.*

shop in Bear Street, I spoke to his mother Joan about her life in Barnstaple with her husband Cyril, who died in 1998. Cyril was an enthusiastic sportsman who achieved a great deal in his specialised sport of swimming, which I will cover later in the book.

Joan was earning 7s.6d. a week as a cashier in Timothy White's chemists when she first met Cyril who was working across the road in Halfords. They both belonged to the Barnstaple Imperial Wheelers Club and it was not long before they were dating. When cash registers were introduced into the shop Joan's job came to an end. Her next job was in the licensing trade with wine and spirit merchants Dennings in the High Street. Joan told me that no women were allowed in the bar but they could use the Jug and Bottle, which was a small area with no seats, and even then they could only have one drink. It was a case of 'Don't sit down, you're not stopping'!

Joan and Cyril married in 1942 when Cyril was in the RAF. In 1946 he returned home and went back to work at Halfords. While waiting in the barbers for a haircut one day Cyril was approached by Archie Jones who ran a cycle and pram shop in High Street. He offered Cyril a job if he could improve the turnover of the business. Cyril took up the offer and promptly improved sales.

Charlie Bradden was the bicycle repair man and worked in the room at the back of the shop. Later Mike Bond joined the business and also repaired bikes and prams. Archie is remembered for never throwing anything away – labels, string, paper and anything that could have further use. Staff had to write in pencil so it could be rubbed out and the paper reused.

Chris Jones, Archie's grandson, believes that his grandfather was a racing cycle champion and also recalls him as a popular local entertainer.

In 1951 Joan joined the business and with Archie

Jones' daughter-in-law, Isis, started up a baby and children's department. Then in 1956 Cyril and Joan were offered the business in Bear Street and Cyril Webber's Cycle Shop was born.

Archie Jones did a deal with Cyril that he would give up selling bikes if Cyril did not sell prams and if he took Mike Bond with him as the repair man. Mike is still there at the time of writing.

Cafés & Restaurants

I have already mentioned Bromley's and Pearce's restaurants so will concentrate on several other eating establishments in the town.

The Central Restaurant was in the High Street between Banbury's and the Guildhall. Arthur Squires told me of its shop at the front where they sold 'the most wonderful pork pies'. Iris Crook worked here as a waitress in 1935 and says that downstairs was a restaurant, which at the back had a long table where all the farmers would congregate on market days. There were also 22 bedrooms, the usual customers being commercial travellers. Bed and breakfast was 4s.6d.

Rosie Potter spoke to me about her long and interesting life in our town. She was born Rosina Divito in Montattico, Italy. Her father, Libero, lived with his family in Fife, Scotland, where they had an ice-cream parlour and made their own ice-cream, which they sold from the back of a horse and cart. When they thought it was time for Libero to marry he was sent home to Italy where they had arranged a marriage for him. He wasn't at all pleased with his parents' choice and so found his own wife, Lucia. Libero had to return to Scotland, leaving Lucia behind. Rosina (Rosie) was born nine months later. In the meantime Libero had moved to South Wales in partnership with another Italian in a fish and chip shop.

❧ Eating Out ❧

Left: *In 1900 Mr A.G. Bromley took over Brooks Café where he had been an apprentice. His son Frank enlarged the business in 1924 and grandson Michael later joined his parents in the trade. The shop in High Street was sold to a building society in 1974.*

Above: *Douglas and Rosie Potter after a civic lunch held at the Maris Convent in 1979.*

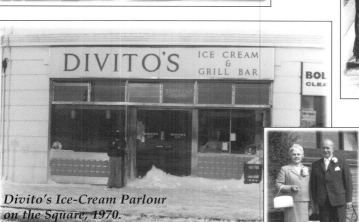

Divito's Ice-Cream Parlour on the Square, 1970.

Right: *Libero and Lucia Divito.*

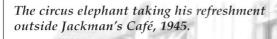

Below: *Jackman's Café, Sticklepath, c.1950.*

The circus elephant taking his refreshment outside Jackman's Café, 1945.

Lucia was not happy with life without her husband and eventually arrived with her baby daughter in Wales where the family was reunited. Over the years the family enlarged with four more daughters, Mary, Rene, Anita and Landa.

It was thought to be more up-market to be the owner of an ice-cream parlour, rather than a fish and chip shop, and the Italian families (in the broad sense of the word) looked out for each other. So Charles Forte, who came from a village three miles from Montattico and knew the Divito family, sent his cousin to help Libero find a suitable business in Taunton where there were properties for sale. The two men travelled across to Ilfracombe by steamer and caught the train to Barnstaple Junction where they had to wait for the connection to Taunton. But Mr Forte had a problem with his internal plumbing and whilst he was in the gentlemen's room their train came and left! The two men had to wait for the next one so they decided to have a look at Barnstaple. Walking around the town they saw a prime property on the Square. Being astute businessmen they forged a deal to buy it. So Taunton's loss became Barnstaple's gain for the young people of the town who spent hours over their frothy coffee, whipped chocolate, ice-cream sundaes and knickerbocker glories. The date was 1939 and the Second World War was about to break out.

Rosie met her husband Douglas when she visited friends Janet and Ada Potter. Dougie was their brother and when he asked Rosie out to a dance at the Forester's Hall she told him that she didn't dance and didn't go out with boys. But she did like swimming. The next time she was at the swimming baths Dougie was there. It was after this meeting that she decided to go to the dance. Of course Doug was there and asked if he could see her home.

Rosie and Doug married in 1950. He was a GPO linesman but later went to work in the café and they moved in above the shop when Libero and Lucia retired. In later years Doug and Rosie opened the Pelican fish and chip shop at the top of Sticklepath Hill. Doug became a town councillor and served as the Mayor of Barnstaple and Chairman of North Devon District Council between 1978 and 1980. Later he was Chairman of Devon County Council.

The ice-cream parlour closed in 1978 but there are still many people who nostalgically remember whiling away their youthful years in Divito's ICP.

Jackman's Café in the High Street had been purchased as a dairy just before the war by Ruby Jackman, but as it was requisitioned during hostilities she bought another dairy at the top of Sticklepath. She soon found there was more profit in running a café so converted the ground floor and put out the 'Open' signs. Their first customers were American soldiers who called Ruby 'Ma Jackman' – a name that stuck with her. For a more detailed description of this era see Chapter Ten.

Ruby and her daughter Monica worked long hours, seven days a week. The only day they closed was Christmas Day and even then a local character, Geordy the tramp, used to come to eat with them. They stayed open all night during the Land's End Trial to serve meals to the competitors. The cars were on their way from Land's End and would start arriving at midnight before going on to the next stage at Beggars Roost on Exmoor.

Monica is also proud that the cyclists' clubs awarded them 'The best café to eat at'. These were touring cyclists, time trialists and road racers who would stay overnight during events. She especially remembers the Corinthians of Plymouth, Imperial Wheelers of Barnstaple and Fred Peters of the South Molton Club who nominated the café as the top place to stop. She says Fred was so keen about his bike that he took it up to the bedroom with him. She said that on occasions they were so crowded with competitors they would sleep four to a bed.

She remembers the elephant that stopped at the café for refreshment. It happened when the circus came to town on a train and moved by road on to Bideford for their show. This meant that many of the animals had to walk. The elephant trainer stopped at Jackman's for a drink and so did the elephant. He had his outside.

Builders

Naturally there have been many building firms in and around the town over the past century and it would be impossible to mention them all, so I will concentrate on those that have given me information.

One of the largest firms was Woolaways, which was established in 1805 when the owners were probably jobbing builders. Later in the century the arrival of the railway presented them with the opportunity to turn their skills to bridge building, such as the Chelfham Viaduct in 1897 and the Kingford road bridge near the Portsmouth Arms on the A377.

Before the First World War the business was in the hands of brothers, William and Fred Woolaway, and through the years the company has been responsible for such projects as the Barnstaple Brick and Tile Company, the building of the Westward Ho! Holiday Camp and a model estate on 40 acres in the Sticklepath area. It is interesting to note that a two-bedroom bungalow on the Oakland Park Estate cost just £630 when it was built in the early 1930s.

Projects built in the early-twentieth century by Woolaways were the Stanbury Flour Mills on Rolle Quay, the Post Office in Cross Street and the electricity power station in Castle Street, all of which no longer exist.

Another building firm in prominence from the 1940s was R. Harris and Son Ltd. Dick Braddon told me that his uncle, Robert Harris, started the business in 1946 and Dick became company secretary and director.

The company constructed housing estates in North Devon as well as larger buildings, such as the Ayres and Grimshaw engineering factory on Braunton Road.

Brian Burgess spent many hours searching out his family's building history, for which I am most grateful. Brian and his brother Clive are the last in a long line of Burgesses in the family business. The two brothers have traced their family back to North Molton in 1529, where John Burgess was a yeoman farmer. The first Burgess to become a builder was Thomas Henry (1831–1907). Clive and Brian's grandfather Henry joined his father's business after a seven-year apprenticeship with Shapland and Petter and he and his wife Agnes purchased 45 Bear Street, which became the builders yard and carpentry shop and also the family home. At one time there was a workforce of 200 men and the only means of transport was by horse and cart. Henry was responsible for many of the buildings which took Barnstaple through the twentieth century.

Not many people know that Burgess erected the wall alongside the river by the Athenaeum, the Bridge Chambers, Victoria Chambers and the Symons building in Boutport Street, which currently houses the Tourist Information office. They built homes in Richmond Street, Fort Street, Alexandra Road and part of Ebberly Lawn. Henry also built the Emmanuel Church in Summerland Street which 99 years later Clive and Brian had the job of demolishing!

It says a great deal of the skills and craftsmanship of Henry Burgess that many of their buildings now have preservation orders on them.

Henry's son Richard Henry, born in 1887, continued his father's business and built Blackmoor Gate Hotel, which was demolished after a fire in the 1960s. He also built large houses at Putsborough, Bickington and the Pickford's Depository in Barnstaple. In the 1920s and '30s he built houses at Yeo Vale and the Rackfield housing estate which included George Street, Coronation Street, King Edward Street and Charles Street.

The firm's account books show that in September 1926 foreman Bill Courtney earned £2.18s. for a 50-hour week and Mr Suffolk, a carthorse driver, earned £1.10s. Arthur Roulstone, a carpenter and joiner, earned £2.1s. and a labourer's wage was 16s.6d.

Clive and Brian Burgess became directors of the family business and carried on their forefathers' tradition in house building developing many more estates in the town and surrounding area. In the 1970s and '80s the firm specialised in quality restoration and renovation of some of North Devon's finest buildings. In 1963 they opened one of the first DIY shops in Barnstaple at their Bear Street premises. The brothers have now retired and the building firm has closed.

Although Norman Brooks spent many years as a policeman, his first trade was as a painter and decorator, serving a five-year apprenticeship with Phillips of Bear Street. He worked on churches and big houses in the town. They also had a contract to paint the houses in Ceramic Terrace, which was owned by Brannam's Pottery. He worked on the Maris Convent before it was a school, North Devon Infirmary, the Children's Home and 19 Alexandra Road, which was the workhouse but, according to Norman, they always had to refer to it as 19 Alexandra Road.

Carpenters outside the workshop of Burgess the builders in Bear Street, 1905. Henry Burgess is pictured second on the right.

Left: *Clive and Brian Burgess arrange the demolition of the Emmanuel Church in Summerland Street 99 years after their grandfather Henry built it.*

Right: *Builder Fred Offield shows Keith Abraham the nineteenth-century tile-making machine he found in his builders yard in 1960. He later gave it to the Barnstaple Museum.*

Norman remarks that there was no scaffolding in those days and to get high up on buildings they had to tie long ladders together and climb them very carefully. The same went for climbing over roofs. He remembers using this tied-ladder method when painting the rear of the Imperial Hotel in Litchdon Street. When he started in the trade there were also no ready-mixed paints or colour charts. They had to mix their own and it took an experienced painter to mix a second amount of paint and get the same shade as the first.

Norman did not have much call for his wallpapering skills as there was very little wallpaper available after the war. But he does recall having to push all their decorating equipment around Barnstaple in a handcart. The ladders would be laid on the cart and paint pots and tools would hang from them.

Funeral Directors

After several conversations with Frank and Jo Simmonds I feel I could write a book entitled 'Tales of an Undertaker', because for such a solemn occupation undertakers seem to have the most glorious sense of humour.

Frank Simmonds was born in 1925, the younger of twins – his sister Edith Maud is 20 minutes older than him. Their parents were Albert and Mary and later along came siblings Fred, Elizabeth, Jim, Jo and Dan. With his five sons Albert made up the business of A.G. Simmonds & Sons, Builders and Funeral Directors. In 1941, at the age of 17, Frank says that he was the youngest funeral director in the country. Here are a few of his memories of the undertaking business:

Mr Chilcott of Litchdon Street Dairy had a horse called Peggy, which was stabled in the Simmonds' yard and there was an agreement between Albert Simmonds and Mr Chilcott that they could use Peggy for funerals to pull the hearse. On one occasion, Peggy was waiting with the hearse outside a house in Broadfield Road and the wreaths were laid on top of

the hedge before the coffin was brought out. Peggy obviously got bored with the proceedings and whiled away her time sampling the floral tributes!

Another story told to me by Frank's brother Jo was of the morning they opened the doors to the stable yard to find Peggy spread-eagled over a huge hole in the ground. During the night a drain had collapsed under the horse and it was too petrified to move. They eventually got Peggy out of the yard but she refused ever to go back again.

Frank told me of a time when he had to keep his sense of humour under strict control. An elderly man had passed on and Frank had removed the body to the Chapel of Rest. That evening there was a tap at his door and when he opened it he saw that it was the deceased's daughter. She said she'd come about her father. Frank assumed she wished to see him laid at rest and asked, 'Do you want to see father? He really looks quite nice.' 'No,' she said, 'I don't want to see him. It's about father's teeth.' Now, before removing the body from the house Frank had been given the old man's teeth to put in when preparing him for burial. 'Oh, yes,' said Frank. 'I've put them in.' 'Well, you'll have to take them out Mr Simmonds; there's been a mistake. We've given you mother's teeth and she can't eat her dinner!'

Jo also told me about the absent-minded parson who after a funeral was searching the car park for his vehicle. When Jo asked him what he was looking for he replied, 'I can't remember where I left my car.' Jo said, 'At home, I should think Vicar, as you came on your bike!'

Perhaps it was the same clergyman who after following the bereaved outside the church was asked by Jo if he had to leave his gardening in a hurry. 'How did you know I'd been gardening?' enquired the cleric. 'Well Vicar, you've still got your Wellingtons on!'

It is meeting people like Frank and Jo during my research for this book that has made the whole process such a pleasure.

Albert Simmonds taking his children, baby Elizabeth and twins Edith and Frank, for an outing on his motorbike and sidecar.

Vets

You cannot class vets as trades people but this seems to be the best place to write about my discussions with Dudley Pettett and Jenny Watts, who came to Barnstaple in 1963 to work for Dudley at his practice at Rumsam. Jenny says she was the first woman vet in North Devon. There were only two practices in Barnstaple at the time: Pettetts, with Dudley Pettett and Ken George as partners; and Coward, Graves and Kingsbury at Pilton.

Jenny arrived to a baptism of fire because it was the freezing winter of 1963 and she had to cover nearly all of North Devon from the edge of Exmoor almost to the Cornwall border. She recalls a blizzard at Blackmoor Gate where she had to drive through a tunnel of snow to get to a farm.

Dudley took Jenny on his rounds to meet farmers who were sceptical about the abilities of a woman vet. However, it was lambing time and they found that a little lady with small hands could get into places where men's large hands could not and save ewes who were in trouble. When Dudley had shown Jenny the ropes he decided he could take a day off. Jenny was left in charge and went happily on her rounds. While she was driving to Umberleigh the practice car coughed and spluttered to a halt. It had run out of petrol! She says she hadn't realised that being North Devon's first woman vet meant she also had to remember to fill the car with petrol.

Dudley Pettett on the left, as a student at Seale Hayne Agricultural College, 1936.

Dudley Pettett was born in Plymouth and after studying at Seale Hayne Agricultural College and Liverpool University, where he qualified as a veterinary surgeon, he returned to Plymouth to work. But the bombing of that city during the war forced the practice to close and Dudley had to look elsewhere. So it was that he and his wife Ina came to Barnstaple in 1942, where he joined Captain Webb who was a Ministry vet with a practice in Joy Street and was about to retire. Four years later he retired and Dudley took over the practice.

Percy Penhale had a practice next to the old Police Station in Castle Street. Pettett and Penhale were the only vets in practice in this area, covering the huge area between Barnstaple and Minehead, and Crediton in the other direction. Dudley said

there were plenty of 'donkey doctors' (unqualified vets) about but very few proper ones.

In 1945 Dudley and his wife Ina found Ashcroft at Rumsam, where they could have kennels as well as Dudley's general practice. He has now retired but his son Richard and daughter-in-law Judith carry on a practice that has one other full-time and three part-time vets, plus five veterinary nurses.

Dudley has a repertoire of stories. He started by telling me that during the Second World War Captain Webb, as a responsible citizen, was delegated to run to the Parish Church and toll the bell in the event of Barnstaple being invaded by the Germans!

Gordon Potter was the blacksmith at Challacombe. The blackout was on and the cars had their headlights masked with slits so that any enemy planes couldn't see them. The problem was that it cut visibility to about 10 yards! Gordon phoned 'Webby' one evening and said, 'Captain, I think my mare's got colic. Can you come out?' 'It's a hell of a way to come, and it'll take ages to get there,' replied Webb. 'Have you got any whisky?' 'Well, funny thing, I got half a bottle at the Ring o' Bells last night.' Captain Webb told Dudley to get the equipment together and they drove the 12 miles to Challacombe. It took quite some time. When they arrived Gordon said to 'Webby', 'She's down in the shed by the bridge.' He lit a hurricane lamp, gave it to Captain Webb and they all went to the shed. Gordon looked over the door and said with surprise, 'I think she looks a bit better.' Webb examined the horse, prodded it here and prodded it there, listened to its heart and guts and said, 'Have you given it anything?' 'Yes,' replied Gordon, 'the whisky, like you said.' 'You fool, that was for me!' retorted Captain Webb.

Gordon Potter had a trainee apprentice named Dick Rawle and in those days vets carried around a whole chemist shop in the back of the car so they could make up medicines for the animals. At this time there was a lot of flu about and Dick Rawle was feeling pretty rough with it. Dick asked Dudley if he'd got anything in his chemist box to help him over this bout of flu. Dudley was carrying some Clorodine (a mixture which was popular before the war and tasted rather pleasant) and one of the ingredients was morphine.

The veterinary dose was of course stronger than the human dose. Dudley made up an amount of the potion suitable for human consumption, gave it to Mrs Potter and told her to tell the afflicted to take it three times a day. It seems that Dick thought it tasted lovely and it made him so much better that he swigged the whole bottle! He began to feel drowsy so he went to the back of the blacksmiths and fell asleep on a bag of horse nails. They couldn't wake him up for 24 hours!

When Jenny Watts was new at the practice and on duty one snowy winter's day she got a call from Sir Frederick Fowkes, asking if she could help him with a difficult calving case. After about an hour Sir Fred phoned up to ask if anyone was coming. On hearing that Jenny had left a while ago Sir Fred and his 'man' went looking for her and found her with her car, which had slid off the road into a snowdrift. When they got this little slip of a girl back to the farm she couldn't reach the cow and they had to hoist her up onto a bale of straw so that she was on a level with the animal's business end.

Last, but by no means least, Dudley told me about the bulldog clamp. This is a ring-type clamp, put into the noses of cattle to hold them still while carrying out treatment. Dudley was at Arlington injecting cattle and was having trouble with them so he said to the farmer, 'Hold on a minute I'll go to the car and get a bulldog.' The farmer, aghast, said, 'Don't bring a dog out 'ere. Us has got enough trouble already.'

Photographers

In the early part of the twentieth century home photography was still in its infancy and the photographic studios were very popular. You could go along in your best attire and sit poised on a chair or bench with a scenic backdrop behind and have your photograph taken. The picture could then be sent to loved ones to be treasured (and hopefully kept for posterity for people like me who value them greatly for compiling the history of a local area).

In this book there are many photographs which were taken by R.L. Knight, who must be rated as one of North Devon's most talented scenic photographers. We have much to thank him for in his collection of black and white and sepia photographs taken in and around Devon in the first part of the 1900s. The third generation of this photographic family is grandson Stephen, who specialises in wedding photography and has also catalogued R.L. Knight's work, which he reproduces at his studio in Bear Street.

Ralph Lethbridge Knight was born in Dorset in 1886 and probably learnt his trade when working for a professional photographer in Ireland. He came to Barnstaple and took over the photographic businesses of Britton and Major, Darker and Loraine. In 1912 he and his younger brother Coke opened a studio in the High Street (where the Marks and Spencer store stands at the time of writing) but soon afterwards Coke went off to America.

During the First World War Ralph joined the Royal Flying Corps, leaving the business in the very capable hands of his fiancée Nellie Tucker, who was an artist and readily took to photography. When they married in 1920 the bridegroom took his own photographs with a self-constructed timing device which allowed him to rejoin the group before the camera activated. This was no mean feat with 80 guests lined up on the lawns of the Imperial Hotel and Ralph needing to place himself in the middle of the party next to his bride.

Denis Knight, Ralph's son, remembers when he was four years old and his father used the delayed timing device for the family group photograph at his grandparents Tuckers' fiftieth wedding anniversary celebrations in 1926. Denis said they all had to stay in the same positions after the photograph was taken while his father developed the plate in case he needed to get a second shot. He remembers how

Ralph Knight with his wife Nellie and son Denis in his Clyno motor car.

Left: *The shop on the right of the picture was Britton's Photographers, c.1890. It was here that Charles Brannam worked part time for his brother-in-law William Britton.*

R.L. Knight in the rear of the biplane in which he took many aerial photographs.

R.L. Knight in later life, enjoying messing about on the river.

Left: *A sample of Ralph Lethbridge Knight's work with this artistic study of three men around the Tome Stone in Queen Anne's Walk.*

Right: *Tony Freeman off to another photo assignment.*

they all cheered when his father put his head around the darkroom door to announce that the first shot was a success.

Ralph was a keen motorcyclist and would tour the countryside with his wife and Denis in the sidecar, surrounded by his photographic equipment. In the years between the wars Ralph was a familiar figure throughout North Devon, photographing views of the countryside and town. I believe his photography has a natural awareness of the Devonshire way of life, coupled with artistic interpretation.

Another of Ralph's passions was flying and with his friend Bob Boyd, who started Atlantic Coast Airlines at Chivenor in 1934, they would fly up and down the coast in a de Havilland Gypsy Moth biplane. Their aerial photography has left us with an excellent historical record of the town. These aeronautical adventures also led to Ralph's first newspaper scoop in 1938 when the ship the *Carmine Filomena* ran aground off Rat Island, Lundy. The *Daily Mail* rang him and said that if he could get a photograph they would pay all expenses. The two men took off from Chivenor in the late morning in a force-eight gale but found it calmer on the lee of the island, so with careful manoeuvring by the pilot Ralph was able to get a first-class shot of the crippled vessel. After landing, Ralph had to race back to the studio to

develop his one and only photograph and then drive to Plymouth to send it by wire to London. Denis said his father was never one to boast of his achievements but did tell his wife, who told all her friends so they could buy the newspaper next day with Ralph's perfect photograph splashed across the front page.

In more modern times many news events have been captured by our own Barnstaple-born Tony Freeman. After leaving the North Devon Technical College Tony served a five-year apprenticeship with Bowdens Photographic. He says that along with being taught the basics of the profession he learnt how to work at speed. It stood him in good stead for his appointment as the youngest photographer to work in a regional newspaper office at the *Express and Echo* and *Western Times*. He stayed with them for 14 years where he came into contact with Fleet Street and television journalism when it was in its infancy.

As a freelance photographic journalist Tony has travelled the globe and flown in every kind of air transport from hang-gliders to jet fighters. He has worked with movie cameras and taken pictures for newspapers, magazines and television. He has met the rich and famous but has resisted offers to move to other parts of the world. What better place to live than in North Devon, he says, where you can be on the beach or the moor and yet get to work within minutes.

~§ Garages §~

Left: *The Trafalgar Cycle Works in 1910, where Sidney Bale sold Royal Enfield bicycles. Sidney was the first to sell automobiles in the town after which the name of the business was changed to The Barnstaple Motor and Cycle Works. Cecil his son joined him in the business and they moved to the prominent position on the Square.*

Right: *Prideaux Garage and Motor Works in Bear Street, c.1910.*

Below: *Bale's Garage on the Square in 1926.*

❧ Town Trades ❧

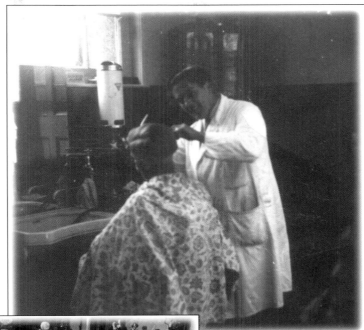

Right: *Barber Alfred Harris in his shop in Vicarage Street.*

Left: *Fred Edmonds, a well-known figure in the town who worked as a barber in his shop behind Cooks sweet shop in the High Street. This photo was taken after a wager between Fred and farmer Charlie Coats. Charlie bet that he could shear a sheep quicker than Fred could cut a head of hair. Fred won by a hair!*

Right: *Raymond Gale, who repaired all types of boots and shoes with the help of his wife in their shop in Paternoster Row until they retired in 2001.*

❧ Town Trades ❧

Above: *Summerland Street General Store, 1910. The Wallis family outside their shop before the baptism of their new son, Norton Wallis.*

Left: *Dymonds, the fish and poultry merchants in Boutport Street.*

Right: *Lewis & Sons Removers, est. 1835, by Edward Lewis at 8 Silver Street. The family business is currently run by Simon (fifth generation) with the help of his father David. In the early days Lewis' were also upholsterers and cabinet-makers. Horse-drawn vehicles were used for removals and later longer distances were undertaken by rail. In 2002 they travel to international destinations. This photograph was taken at the 1933 Carnival. Fifth from the left is William Lewis, son of the original owner. Far right is William's son Edward.*

Chapter Nine

THE MILLENARY CELEBRATIONS

In 1930 Barnstaple celebrated 1,000 years as a borough. The Mayor and Corporation arranged celebrations to commemorate this momentous occasion. In the official millenary brochure the author, Francis Gribble, wrote a foreword in which he posed the question: 'Is Barnstaple really the oldest borough in the United Kingdom? There are one or two other claimants; and things which happened 1,000 years ago, both in Barnstaple and elsewhere, are now wrapped in the clouds of obscurity.' It would seem that even then there was some doubt as to the authenticity of the claim of a Royal Charter being granted to the town in AD930. But whatever the arguments for and against, Barnstaple's long history and proud heritage surely gave townspeople every right to celebrate as they did in the summer of 1930.

Right: A large crowd gather to watch the Mayor John Trump Dunn open the swimming baths in Rock Park.
Photograph R.L. Knight.

Below: Children playing on the newly opened boating pond near the swimming baths.
Photograph R.L. Knight.

The brochure sets out the plans, centred on Rock Park which was to have an open-air swimming pool, children's boating lake and tennis courts. A simple inscribed block of granite was placed in a paved area surrounded by a yew hedge. There was also to be a sundial, which was being provided by the grammar school.

The celebrations started on Saturday 9 August with a carnival on the River Taw and in the evening the boathouse and boats were lit with coloured lights. The next day thanksgiving services were held in the various churches in the town, followed in the afternoon by an open-air service in the park with massed choirs led by the Band of the 14th Hussars, who later gave a concert in the castle grounds.

On Monday 11 August, Alderman Arthur J. Reavell was presented with the Freedom of the Borough at the Guildhall and there were further concerts by the 14th Hussars. The next day saw sports in the park followed by music from the band of the Devonshire Regiment and the Barnstaple Military Band. A fireworks display was held that evening on Seven Brethren Bank which was watched by crowds in the park across the river. The celebrations concluded on 15 and 16 September when schoolchildren held a pageant on the sports ground in the park depicting 'Barnstaple through the Centuries'.

Left: *Unveiling the millenary stone.*
Photograph R.L. Knight.

Right: *The open-air service in Rock Park on 10 August 1930.*
Photograph R.L. Knight.

Children of St Mary's School in period costume during the millenary celebrations. Some of those included in the photograph are: ? *Coombes and Tom Featherstone, Ken Smith, Len Pickard, Len Richards, Jim Bower, Betty Fewings and George Laity.* Photograph R.L. Knight.

❧ *The Town Celebrates* ❧

Left: *One of the plays by the schoolchildren in the park.* Photograph R.L. Knight.

Right: *The open-air swimming baths, Rock Park, 1930.*

Left: *The Mayor presenting millenary mugs to schoolchildren.*

Right: *Children in procession during their pageant in Rock Park.*

The Town Celebrates

Right: *Freeman of the Borough Dr Edwards planting a beech tree in the Square as part of the celebrations. The tree soon withered and died. The Mayor and others replaced it at the dead of night.* Photograph R.L. Knight.

Above: *Mayor Trump Dunn about to carve a turkey for a dinner at the Children's Institution.* Photograph R.L. Knight.

Right: *The fair procession during the millenary year.* Photograph R.L. Knight.

The Mayor and Mayoress visit North Place, Green Lane where the residents held a street party. Gwendoline Ford is the little girl sitting on a stool on the far right of the picture and her father Albert is standing behind her. She told me that she can remember all the people in this picture.
Photograph R.L. Knight.

Chapter Ten

WARTIME

Above: *Soldiers (possibly the Devon Yeomanry) leaving Barnstaple via the Square and Long Bridge, 1914.*

Right: *Raymond's Bakery bread-van horse was requisitioned during the First World War, 1914.*

The two world wars took Barnstaple's sons and daughters as it took so many from all over Britain and the Commonwealth. The memorial in Rock Park beside the quietly flowing waters of the Taw honours those from Barum who never came back.

The First World War will have occurred a century ago in the not-so-distant future, so the living memories I gathered are from the generation who came after it. Raymond Wickham told me of his father Bill who, with his two brothers George and Fred, went to war, but only Bill returned. Fred was killed at Ypres at the age of 19 and George died in Cologne at the age of 23 (*both boys can be seen in the photograph on page 60*). Another casualty of war was George Hewitt, who grew up never

Reginald Bale, who lived at Newport, was killed in the First World War.

knowing his father as he had answered to the call: 'Your Country Needs You'.

Others welcomed back loved ones whose lives were tragically shattered by what they had endured. They were men such as William Gee, who had been gassed in France, and Alfred Fewings' father Reg, as well as Mary Stribling's father, whose injuries sustained in the Battle of the Somme claimed his life in his early forties.

The battles of the First World War were carried out away from our shores in France and Belgium, but during the Second World War the action came right to our doorstep. For the first time the South West of England suffered badly from enemy bombing with Exeter and Plymouth being blitzed.

The First World War Remembered

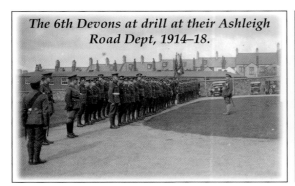

The 6th Devons at drill at their Ashleigh Road Dept, 1914–18.

Mounted soldiers in Bear Street during the First World War.

The Devon Yeomanry outside their headquarters in Tuly Street during the First World War.

Wounded soldiers outside the North Devon Infirmary, 1918.

Barnstaple escaped relatively unscathed, but this war left its mark on the lives of many.

It is a well-known fact that you always remember what you were doing at the time of a momentous occurrence. One such occasion was the radio announcement on Sunday 3 September 1939 that Britain was at war with Germany. Joyce Richards, whose home was in Kent, was staying with family friends Dai and Matty Morgan in Clifton Terrace. Joyce said her parents and brother usually spent their summer holidays with her at the Morgans but on this occasion she was on her own. After the news on the radio, she said, it did not seem long before her brother was on the Morgans' doorstep with his gas mask in his hand. They both still live in the town.

Eric Bennett who lived in Gaydon Street was nine years old and recalls that morning well. He says his father, a keen radio ham, was tuning into different stations all morning in search of the latest news and neighbours crowded around the wireless set in the front room. He says that when the news bulletin came through at 11a.m. people became subdued and left for their homes. He went to Sunday School as usual that afternoon but as there were so few in attendance they were sent home. Mr Seyfert, a naturalised German who ran a wholesale confectionery business from his home at Ebberly Lawn, decided to give away all his ice-cream to the children of the town. Both Eric and Dick Braddon told me that the Seyferts' premises were soon overrun with youngsters.

Sheila Armstrong, née Wilks, said that in 1940 her father George lost his job as a chauffeur due to petrol rationing and so with her parents and younger sister Sylvia they moved to Barnstaple from Kentisbury. George got a job as taxi-driver and serviceman for Hopgoods Garage, which later became Taw Garages. Her mother Betty worked for the war effort at Shapland and Petter making camouflage netting. Sheila's first job was in the office of an aircraft factory at Chivenor Aerodrome, where they made small aircraft. She remembers that the people on the shop floor who worked with 'dope' (a type of glue) were given an extra milk allowance. Sheila said it wasn't all

hard work and no play. She told me of the dances at the Foresters Hall (Iceland at the time of writing), the Assembly Rooms (the Conservative Club at the time of writing) and Bromley's Ballroom. She also loved to go to Divito's Ice-Cream Parlour and often had to queue up as it was frequently full of American soldiers. She recalls the wonderful ice-cream sodas, hot chocolate and knickerbocker glories for 2s.6d.

Rosie Divito was 12 years old when the war broke out and her parents had only just taken over possession of the ice-cream parlour on the Square. The parlour became a second home to American and Italian troops. Rosie remembers her mother Lucia's pleasure in cooking macaroni for them. Lucia never really learnt the language of her adopted country although, said Rosie, she knew how to count the money. Occasional fracas would break out in the café when it was full of Americans. On one occasion five-foot-nothing Rosie stood between two soldiers, both in excess of six feet, and held them apart whilst reading them the 'riot act'. When the soldiers were leaving the area their commanding officer came to the café and asked if it had been 'liberated' of any property, but the only things missing were the metal stands the glass coffee mugs stood in. Boxes of them were returned! Rosie still has a few today.

The Americans certainly seem to have made their mark on the town. Brian Burgess also recalls an American couple, Mr and Mrs St Ledger-Barter, who were marooned over here during the war. He had been in the United States Air Force, so he joined the Royal Air Force, and she nursed at Fremington Army Camp. Brian told me about the bumper ration boxes the couple gave to him and to his brother Clive. There were tins of meat, biscuits, cake, boiled sweets, chocolate (all rare treats for two British lads at the time) and, lastly, condoms! The boys blew them up and used them as balloons or water bombs.

Another haunt of the American servicemen was Jackman's Café at Sticklepath. They called Ruby Jackman 'Ma'. Her daughter Monica said that one Sunday they were cleaning the café and the Americans came in and asked for food, so with her mother she prepared full English breakfasts with two eggs on

Foot-soldiers marching over Long Bridge during the Second World War.

Boy Scout evacuees marching along the Strand, c.1939.

Barnstaple's Second World War

Above: *Atlantic Coast Airlines staff,
Fairview, 1941.*

Below: *Soldiers marching across the Square
during the Second World War.*

Above: *Barnstaple Accordion Band, who played for many of the dances and
socials during wartime. (Note the misspelling on their banner.)*

Below: *The Albert Hall as it stood the morning
after the wartime fire that gutted the building
in 1941. The notice at the front of the building
is advertising 'Dance Tonight'.*
Photograph R.L. Knight.

Above: *The Devonshire Regiment Band, 1931.
Third from left, back row: Frederick Gee. He
joined the regiment at the age of 17 and saw
action at the siege of Malta and then
in Sicily. He was killed in action in France
on 19 June 1944.*

toast, chips, bacon, chops, tomato and toast plus two glasses of milk, apple pie and ice-cream – all for 2s.6d.! It is not surprising that Jackman's Café won a reputation for being a good place to eat during those war years. Monica told me that Liberty trucks would bring the Americans into town on their pay nights and drop them off at the café. The men would have a coffee and then go off to enjoy a night on the town, returning to the café for a meal later. The noise of the men and their trucks disturbed some residents and moves were made to make the café 'off limits'. However, the commanding officers of the military camps at Instow, Fremington and Chivenor decided against this as they felt that the café, Ruby and Monica were doing a good service by keeping up the troops' morale.

The Americans were billeted in houses around the town. Many lived at Ebberly Lawn and the Symons Hotel in Boutport Street was requisitioned for them. Dudley Pettett remembers those who lived at the Waverly Hotel on the corner of High Street and Joy Street and how they lined up for 'roll call' each morning before marching off to the Square.

Eric Bennett says that in 1943, when there were thousands of American troops in North Devon, he went with his pals to see the tanks, landing craft, lorries and jeeps parked on North Walk. They had a band and would march to the Square every morning and raise the Stars and Stripes on their headquarters in the building on the corner of Boutport Street and the Square (a wine bar at the time of writing).

Keith James lived at Congrams Close during the war and his earliest memories are of when he was barely two years old and his father ferried aircraft parts from Chivenor to the Midlands. Keith and his mother went along to keep him company on the long journey. Keith sat on a makeshift seat made out of a fire-guard between his parents in the lorry cab. He also remembers the American soldiers at the Symons Hotel. He told me that when they left and the building was renovated, several articles were found under the floorboards,

Dick Raymond, who joined the RAF in 1942 and became a flight engineer on Bomber Command. He was badly injured when a Lancaster bomber exploded at RAF Wyton and when he returned to duty he found that all his crew had been killed on flying missions. Dick's aircraft was later shot down over Holland and four of the seven crew were killed. Dick spent a harrowing year as a prisoner of war at Stalag Luft 7, Upper Silesia, Germany. In January 1945 he was forced to march away from the camp with 1,550 other prisoners.

including a crocodile carved from an elephant's tusk, an American bugle and a toy gun which fired pellets made from newspaper. Keith became the proud owner of this memorabilia and regrets that he sold them for £8 to buy a fishing rod!

Although Barnstaple became fully involved in the preparations for the hostilities it suffered little enemy action. One night the town was rocked when a German bomber tried to demolish the Newport side of the town. It is thought that the target was the gasometer in Barbican Road, but thankfully the person aiming the bomb was not on his best form. The first bomb partly demolished a house in Chester Terrace and the other fell in a garden in Portmore Lane.

Another wartime incident involved an Anson bomber which was stationed at Chivenor. Eric Bennett was in the school gardens in Vicarage Street and saw the plane losing height in the Shirwell direction. It hit the ground in the field above where the North Devon District Hospital is at the time of writing and careered across the field and the road until it hit the wall of Raleigh Park. Cecil Gammon's father was driving his lorry home to Milltown and stopped to pass the time of day with his friend Sidney Pratt, who was working as a lengthman on the road by Raleigh Park. Ernie bade his friend goodnight and moved off for home. He had gone only a few yards when the aircraft slewed across the road behind him, killing his friend. Ernie would often tell this story and how the heat from the blast melted the tyres on his lorry.

Talking of explosions reminded me of the story Joan Webber told me of her wartime job with Atlantic Coast Airlines in a large garage at the back of Fairview. They rebuilt damaged wooden gliders which were used to drop our soldiers over enemy lines. One day when painting the wings of a plane they accidentally set fire to the paint. The employees escaped but the building burned down. New premises were found at the Corona Works in Newport. Joan told me that to celebrate victory on VE Day the workforce took chisels to the glider they had just completed.

There were many street parties and celebrations on Victory in Europe Day. In Derby the houses were painted red, white and blue and festooned with decorative streamers. Trestle-tables were erected down the centre of the streets and tea was laid out for the children. Streets competed with each other to see who could put on the best display. Ernie Ovey remembers that Charlie Symons' Accordion Band played all night on a stage set up at the bottom of Newington Street.

Land Army girls. Queenie Ovey, Dorie Geen, Elsie Worker, Florrie Guard, Marge Passmore and Norah Williams.

The British Restaurant in what is the Queen's Theatre at the time of writing is another wartime memory etched on people's minds. I have often been told of the fire in 1941, which destroyed the building and left only the retaining walls. The upstairs had housed the Albert Hall theatre and dance hall. Downstairs was the Corn Market, which was being used to store foodstuffs and unfortunately highly inflammable sugar was part of these stores. Harold Mock, who was a fireman at the time, says the blaze was uncontrollable by the time the brigade arrived. The British Restaurant was also on the ground floor. Later the whole building was rebuilt as the Queen's Hall and opened in 1953.

Keith James recalls how his grandmother would collect him from the cinema on Saturday morning and take him to the British Restaurant, where they would have lunch for 1s.9d. They were given different coloured counters for each course. Keith's favourite was treacle pudding with lashings of custard running down the side. He was always treated to his grandmother's ice-cream on top of his pudding. Keith says he has retained his sweet tooth!

Many of these stories seem light-hearted but I am sure that is the stoic nature of our countrymen. We only retell the happy or funny occasions. My parents experienced the horrors of the Blitz in London but I can only remember the hilarious stories they would recount as we sat around the dinner table on a Sunday. It was due to those devastating war years that they moved to Barnstaple where they had spent many happy holidays. As petrol was rationed their mode of transport from London to Barnstaple during the war was a tandem bicycle!

Right: *Home Guard unit outside Ashleigh Road Drill Hall.* Fourth from left in the front row: *Major Manaton, editor of the* North Devon Journal.

Below: *Outside Ashleigh Road Drill Hall, 1939/45.*

Bottom right: *Home Guard marching from Queen Street into Boutport Street, 1944.*

✂ VE Day ✂

Above: 2. Mrs Langley's lodger, 3. Mr Ridd, 4. Mr Gilbert, 5. Mrs Ridd, 7. Bert Balch, 8. Gwen Brend,
10. Florence Popham, 11. Mrs Gould, 12. Mrs Brend, 13. Pearl Adams, 14. Mrs Balch, 15. Mrs Lake,
16. Joyce Adams, 17. Mrs Gilbert, 18. Edwin Popham, 19. Amy Ridd, 22. John Howard,
23. Mrs E.V. Howard, 25. Terence Paddon, 26. Ethel Pickard, 27. Leonard Pickard, 29. Mrs Adams,
31. Emily Hopkins, 34. Sylvia Hughes, 36. Doreen Robinson, 38. Sylvia Pickard, 40. Alan Paddon,
42. Keith Lake, 43. Tony Lake, 44. Bill Miles, 46. Connie Barnes, 48. Dennis Hughes,
51. Joan Woollacott, 53. Mrs Ford, 54. Florrie Paddon, 55. Heather Paddon, 56. Mrs Jeffrey,
57. Ronnie Pearson, 58. Sheila Pickard, 61. John Rowe, 63. Pamela Adams, 65. Marjorie Paddon.

❧ VE Day ❧

Queen Street residents.

Lansdown Terrace,
Yeo Vale Road.

Below: *Programme of a wartime concert staged by the Home Guard.*

Above: *Charles Street. Faces in the crowd include Beattie Pile, Gillian Pile, Neil Bartlett, Mr Earl, Julie Marles, Marianne Cook, Gertie Tubbs, Doris Bartlett, Lil Hill, Phil Budd, Audrey Bosence, Margaret Tamlyn, Rose Tamlyn, Lil Withers, John Cook, Mrs Beer, Victor Barlett, Roger and Diane Bosence and Wendy Tubbs.*

Silver Street.

Chapter Eleven

HEALTH CARE

Above: *The Alexandra Hospital.*

Left: *Residents of the borough workhouse (later the Alexandra Hospital).*

A small chapel in the corner of the site which is now occupied by a large complex of retirement flats overlooking the inner relief road is a lasting reminder of where Barnstaple's town workhouse, and then the Alexandra Hospital, once stood.

Before the Welfare State took on the responsibility of the sick and elderly each parish looked after those who were too old, ill or infirm to care for themselves. For the destitute their last hope, and the one they all dreaded, was the Union Workhouse.

Until the National Health Service was established in 1948, a trip to the doctor and any medication or treatment that followed had to be paid for by the patient. Friendly Societies and Benefit Clubs came into being and in 1830 there were up to 12 in the town. One of these was the Loyal Union Society which had 74 members who each contributed 1s.1d. a month. When unable to work through illness they got 5s. a week or double that amount if confined to bed. At the age of 70 an annual payment of £8.8s. was received, which rose to £10 at the age of 75. On death the surviving relative would receive £3.10s. This was the equivalent of sick benefit and life insurance. Those without work or any other means of support had to rely on the parish for money to feed themselves and their families. Anyone on poor relief was not allowed to travel outside the parish bounds without written permission.

In 1834 the Poor Law Institution, or Union Workhouse, was built in Alexandra Road with accommodation for the destitute and offices where the relieving officer and poor law guardians managed the funds. The workhouse had long- and short-stay facilities and some maternity beds. Also provided were a row of small single cells with just a bench to sleep on for vagrants and a padded cell for 'lunatics'! It was the duty of the relieving officer and general practitioners to certify the mentally ill and have them removed to the county mental hospital at Exminster. Cases of epilepsy, or even girls with an illegitimate child, could warrant admission to a mental institution. In 1902 a home for the children of those in the workhouse was built on the opposite side of Alexandra Road.

When the National Health Service was set up the workhouse was closed. However, I am told that out of the Alexandra Hospital's five wards and 120 beds, which were mainly for the elderly and convalescent, there remained a ward known as 'Part 3' – the workhouse ward.

I asked Peggy Rogers, who was a sister at the 'Alex' in the early 1950s, about the inmates of the Part 3 ward and she told me they were 'the down-and-outs who slept rough in shop doorways in the town.' She said that the Police would bring them to the ward where they could have a bath and bed. They had to work for their keep by chopping wood, peeling vegetables or mopping floors.

Dr Eric Lynsey was a medical officer for the hospital in 1965 and remembers his work there with much pleasure. He told me that he enjoyed caring for the elderly people (whom he fondly named his 'antiques'), making sure they were well looked after and kept active in mind as well as body, with the aim of returning them to their own homes. In 1970 Dr Lynsey became a full-time geriatric consultant at the North Devon District Hospital.

Norman Brooks, who often worked as a painter in the 'Alex', says the atmosphere was eerie and the building had long wards and iron staircases. The hospital closed its doors on a long history of caring for the community in 1978 but unfortunately it never lost the black cloak of its nineteenth-century poverty-ridden roots and was still thought of as the workhouse by the elderly of the town. It was later demolished and imposing retirement flats built in its place. Only the original chapel remains.

In 2002 the community's health care is centred on the North Devon District Hospital, overlooking the town at Raleigh Park. It is far removed from its predecessor, the North Devon Infirmary, which was built by voluntary contributions at the end of Barbican Lane facing onto Litchdon Street. Finance was a problem from the time it was established in 1824 and funds were raised by means of bazaars, exhibitions, church services and donations from the wealthy. The original building was quite small and only held 20 beds until two other wings were added. A separate isolation hospital was later opened in Castle Street for people with contagious illnesses such as tuberculosis. It was here that Alfred Fewings' mother Florrie worked (see photograph on page 127).

A fascinating insight into the work of the medical practitioners of the town from the mid-nineteenth

Left: *Staff of the 'Alex' waiting for the arrival of the Duchess of Gloucester who visited the hospital in 1949. Left to right: Lesley Enfield (Group Secretary), ?, ?, Kathleen Miller, Stanley Thorne, Sheila ?, Sylvia Wilks, David Sinden, Marjorie Benstead, John Foster, Micky Leech, Connie Lock, ?, Vera Lugg. The name of the lady on the seat is unknown.*

Right: *Alexandra Court, the residential flats that replaced the old workhouse. The chapel on the left is the only building remaining from those dark days.*

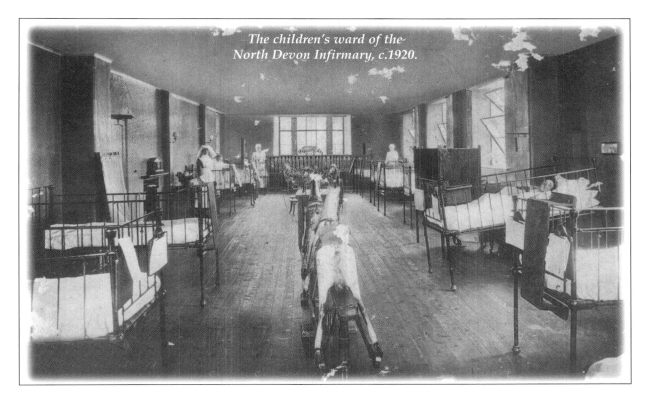

The children's ward of the North Devon Infirmary, c.1920.

century is given in an account of the Bear Street Surgery, written by one of the partners, Dr Gordon Brook, and also in a book written by Mrs Margery Harper about the life of her husband, Dr Richard Harper (referred to by his patients as Uncle Dick), another of the partners. This is the oldest GPs' practice in the town and originated in 1864 when Dr Joseph Harper went into partnership with Dr Charles Morgan. During much of the following 100 years the doctors had consulting rooms in Bear Street before the practice moved to a purpose-built health centre in Vicarage Street in 1975. They shared this building with the Litchdon Street practice. Although both have now moved, their older patients still refer to them by the original names; Bear Street or Litchdon Street Surgeries.

In all, Joseph and Augusta Harper had 13 children and their eldest son John joined his father at the practice in 1894 after training at St Thomas' Hospital in London – the first of many partners down the years to do so. In those early days the doctors carried out their house visits by horse. These visits took them as far away as Braunton and Exmoor. John Harper would go out with lunch and drugs packed into his saddle-bags and would often join the hunt for an hour if he came across them whilst on his rounds! Later, when automobiles provided a different type of horse power, Prideaux, the coach builder further down Bear Street, provided the practice's first vehicle. However, for several years John preferred to continue his night calls around the town on foot rather than trying to kick life into a cold engine with the starting-handle.

The surgery had its own dispensary and Mrs Hall, Mr Hatcher and Wally Youings were employed as dispensers, relieving the doctors of this task. The preparation of powders, ointments and tinctures was done in the Harpers' kitchen amongst the culinary paraphernalia. Mr Hatcher also helped administer anaesthetics and did any other task when the doctor needed another pair of hands. One such occasion was when the local squire fell from his horse on North Walk and broke his leg. Mr Hatcher assisted in setting the injured bone. A surgery boy was also employed. The first one was nine-year-old Reg Litson who would make deliveries around town on a heavy-framed bicycle with a large wicker basket on the front and was paid 1s. a week. Over the years there were a series of surgery 'boys', the last being Mrs Jessie Lakeman, who was not the only female to have done the job. She cycled in from Bradiford twice a day to fetch and carry packages from the surgery to homes around the town.

Dr Brook explained in his history of the practice that in the early 1900s patients paid for their consultations and treatment unless they came under the parish doctor (as previously explained) or they belonged to a club system (as in the Friendly Society). No payment was required at the North Devon Dispensary or the infirmary. The practice bills were made out around the dining-room table and much discussion took place as to the level of fees charged to patients, taking into account their differing circumstances. Country patients paid once a year when they came to Barnstaple Fair. On 'Fair Friday' they would attend the surgery where the doctor would hand them their bill, along with a glass of sherry. They would

⇜ *Old Town* ⇝

Above: *A man washing at the outside tap of one of the houses that were later demolished in the Barnstaple clearances, c.1945.*

Top left: *A young lad sweeping the gulley in the centre of Hardaway Head.*

Left: *Green Lane (now an undercover shopping centre).*

A man and young girl sitting beside the kitchen range, c.1945.

Mrs McWhinnie and Mrs Dunn leading the Red Cross nurses on a church parade in the Square, 1933. These nurses played an important role in both world wars by helping the staff at the infirmary.
Photograph R.L. Knight.

Winners of the Trefisie Cup in 1935. On the back of the card the names are given as Miss Gaydon, Mrs Hollow, Miss Candus, Mrs McWhinnie, Mrs Dunn and Mrs Brindley.
Photograph R.L. Knight.

then go on to visit the rest of the town's merchants where the same process of paying bills and partaking of food and alcoholic refreshment continued!

After the First World War Dr Simeon Shaw was taken on as the fourth partner in the practice. John Harper's son Richard (Dick) became a partner in 1931 and remained there until he retired in 1968. And so the association between the Bear Street Practice and the Harper family came to an end.

During my research I learnt that Dr Richard Harper is remembered with great fondness by all the people who knew him. He showed great kindness and concern for his patients, especially those who lived in the over-crowded and poorly-built houses in the town. He was also a talented photographer and it was through his booklet, *Your Beautiful Town*, which recorded the conditions people lived in, especially in the Derby area, that the Council instigated a rebuilding scheme in the 1950s and '60s.

Patients and staff of the Fever Hospital in Castle Street, 1917. These were tuberculosis patients. Florrie Fewings was one of the nurses.

Dick Harper was also very interested in research and had a laboratory in a small upstairs room at the surgery. He and Drs Gilbert and Brook, who had joined the practice in 1938, worked several nights a week after the surgery closed. There was no other laboratory in North Devon at the time. A blood-transfusion service was arranged at the surgery on a Sunday when the Red Cross would attend and carry out tests for blood grouping. When blood was required at the hospital donors would be called upon to attend for an imme-

diate transfusion. (The National Blood Transfusion Service was later set up during the Second World War.)

In 1946 Dr James Smart joined the practice. During his first winter as a GP in 1947 there was a call from a phone box at Challacombe requesting that he attend to a mother in labour. This was one of the country's most severe winters and Exmoor was a blanket of deep drifts of snow. Dr Smart and Dr Harper set out in two cars but could only get as far as Blackmoor Gate where a guide was waiting for them with two horses. They left their cars and travelled on with Dr Dick on one horse, the guide on the other and Dr Smart on skis. It took over two hours to cover the five miles and reach the isolated farm-house, only to find the baby had already arrived. Today we are safe in the knowledge that the Devon Air Ambulance can reach areas in a few minutes that once took three men, two cars, two horses and a pair of skis many hours!

Many changes occurred over the intervening years, not only with the introduction of the National Health Service but also the working practices of the surgery. Vaccination programmes commenced as diphtheria was still a threat up until the middle of the 1900s. The last epidemic in Barnstaple was in 1942 when there were 22 cases and three deaths. People with serious infectious diseases were sent to the Fever Hospital in Castle Street. Dr Jonas also held a VD clinic at the hospital.

Partners of the Bear Street Surgery take a photocall in the garden of Rackfield House (Dr Harper's home in Boutport Street). Left to right: Dr Lomas, Dr Gordon Brook, Dr Dick Harper, Dr Bradbear, Dr John Harper, Dr Simeon Shaw, Dr K. Saunders.

The present-day partners of Brannam Medical Centre, the direct descendant of the Bear Street practice. Left to right: Registrar Dr Henry Nwosu, Dr Bob Bunney, Dr John Marston, Dr Tom Bigge, Dr Andrew Barbery, Dr Charlotte Mcaie, Dr Iain Stewart, Dr Peter Taylor. Dr Ian Jack is also a partner.

Before the war the partners decided to purchase more sophisticated medical equipment and an electrocardiogram, gastroscope, X-ray machines and anaesthetic equipment were introduced to the practice. All this shows the extent of medical treatment that was carried out in the GPs' surgery. Until the 1950s private operations were carried out by the partners at Beech Hill and Ebberly Lawn Nursing Homes, and they would often start the day in dental surgeries in the town to administer anaesthetics for tooth extractions. Babies were either born at home or at

District Midwife Nurse Wadge with one of 'her' babies.

a private nursing home. The doctor's fee for home deliveries ranged from two to ten guineas. Midwives who attended home births were paid three guineas. The District Midwife in the 1940s was Mrs Lidstone and she was succeeded by Miss Wadge, whom many people still remember cycling on her rounds with her brown leather bag in a wicker basket on the front. After the introduction of the National Health Service the Highfield Nursing Home opened, to which GPs could send patients for their confinement. Complicated cases were taken to the infirmary.

In 1946 Dr Eric Lindsay and his wife Hilda arrived in Barnstaple and Eric took up the position of 'Assistant with a View' (to a partnership) with Dr Acheson at his practice at Choweree, a house on the corner of Boutport Street and Vicarage Street. Like the doctors at the Bear Street practice, before the NHS Dr Lindsay was not only a GP but also an honorary at the infirmary where, along with Dr Smart, he was an anaesthetist (an honorary was an unpaid post at the hospital). I asked Dr Lindsay if he could remember how much people paid for their consultations and medicine before the NHS. He said the doctor's fee was 5s. in cash, which included a bottle of medicine! This came in three different coloured bottles – brown was for a cough, white for indigestion and red was a general tonic. It was 7s.6d. for a home visit by the doctor. If people could not afford to pay he would write out the prescription to take to the Poor Law surgery where the medicine would be dispensed.

Dr Lindsay remembers the severe winter of 1947 and having to travel uphill to Prixford in snow which was so thick that his tyres wouldn't grip, so he took the mats out of his car and put them under the wheels to enable him to move upwards and onwards. He

Dr Eric Lindsay and his wife Hilda receiving gifts after his retirement as Medical Officer for the North Devon Motor Club.

didn't stop to pick them up until on the return journey downhill. He remembers having to deliver babies by candlelight and by the light of a 'Tilly' lantern. On one occasion he was called to a farm as the farmer's daughter wasn't well. When he got there it was obvious the young girl was in the last stages of labour. The farmer and his wife, who lived and worked with the natural elements of life, had no idea that their daughter was about to become a mother.

Eric Lindsay also served with St John Ambulance for 30 years as a Divisional Surgeon and he later became the Area Commissioner.

The Choweree practice was set up in the early 1900s by Dr Manning, who went on his rounds by coach and horses. Dr Hector Acheson came from London to take over this country practice in 1938. Dr Hugh Keatings became a partner with Dr Acheson and Dr Lindsay at the practice in 1955, after 18 months of working as their assistant.

Hugh Keatings first came to Barnstaple during the Second World War when he was stationed at Torquay and with some pals had pooled their petrol coupons and driven up to North Devon in a Ford Poplar for a jaunt. He said he was so taken with the town that he decided he would like to come back here one day to settle down. He recalls Hector Acheson as a rather gruff but kind man who was a very good clinician and teacher. Choweree, he says, was a beautiful Queen Anne building with a two-acre walled garden, which was immaculately kept. The main consulting room was beautifully furnished and would have graced any Harley Street practice, let alone Boutport Street.

Christmas time on the wards, c.1920.

❧ *1940s Nursing* ❧

Above: *Student nurses receiving their certificates at the North Devon Infirmary after their preliminary exams, 1948. Left to right, front row: Peggy Rogers, Barbara Cawley, Winny Stribling, ? Cook.*

Below: *Nurses from the NDI fund-raising for a new hospital, 1947.*

Left: *Christmas time on King George V ward in 1969 (compare this to the 1920 photo).* Left to right: *Mrs Harris, SEN name unknown, Sister Peggy Rogers, Staff Nurse June Hoare, Consultant Mr Stirk, two third-year students and Wendy Clarke.*

Right: *Nursing staff at the Alexandra Hospital, 1969.* Left to right, standing: *Betty Maynard, Margaret Bryant, Staff Nurse ?, Sister Doreen Carter, Staff Nurse Marie Balman, Lil Mallaband, Jean Gratton;* sitting: *Melanie Lawrence, ? Brock.*

Dr Keatings remembers visiting the rows of houses in Derby where, although poverty was rife, there was often a roaring fire in the Bodley with a kettle on the hob and gleaming brasses along the mantlepiece. He lived with his wife Elizabeth at Victoria Road opposite Highfield Nursing Home and recalls nocturnal walks across the road in dressing gown and slippers to attend a confinement.

When Dr Acheson retired in 1965 the practice amalgamated with the Litchdon Street Surgery where Drs Dixey, King, Killard-Levy and Morrell were partners. The surgery in Litchdon Street was right across the road from the 'homely' NDI. He said he would nip across the road to visit his patients and confer with the consultants, arrange an urgent admission or even attend a post-mortem. He said it gave him the sense of being part of a team and looks back on those days as the best of times for a GP.

There follow several accounts of memories provided by those who worked at the North Devon Infirmary.

Peggy Rogers left school at the age of 15 and went to work for the Fifty Shilling Tailors in the High Street (next to where Somerfield is at the time of writing). Peggy wanted to be a nurse but she had not had a grammar-school education and in those days you had to pay for your training. Then she saw an advertisement for girls to do their nurse training and sent for an application form. She took an entrance exam, which she passed. She started training at Exeter but after two months had lost two stone in weight, which she told me was due to 'starvation and hard work'. Dr Harper, Uncle Dick, wrote her a reference enabling her to change her training to the NDI, where the matron was Miss Wright. Peggy took her finals in November 1950 and became a staff nurse on the children's ward (Victoria Ward).

In 1951 Peggy decided to travel and set her heart on New Zealand. She went on the £10 Assisted Travel Scheme in 1952 to a hospital on South Island, New Zealand. Peggy told me that on 2 June 1953 she stayed up all night with her English friends listening to the broadcast of the coronation.

Peggy returned to Barnstaple at Christmas in 1953 and within a month had started work as a sister at the Alexandra Hospital where the matron was Miss Jane Roberts. The two started the Pupil Nurse Training School at Bideford which took in the NDI, the Alexandra Hospital and Bideford Hospital. Peggy returned to the infirmary in 1961 as a ward sister on King George V ward. She was later on the planning committee for the North Devon District Hospital which opened in 1976.

Another nursing sister with a long history of training and working on the wards of the North Devon Infirmary and Alexandra Hospital is Marie Balman. As a nursing officer in 1977 she also helped commission five medical wards for the North Devon District Hospital. She was born in Clovelly, gained a scholarship to Barnstaple Grammar School and qualified as a nurse in 1956. She told me the rules for the nurses' uniforms were strict and had to pass the approval of the matron. First and second-year students wore butterfly hats and the third years had 'bows and strings' (this was a bow tied under the chin and secured with pins under the hat). First years wore yellow belts and the others green belts. Maria remembers one day when Matron Wright spotted her walking down the corridor and bellowed 'Nurse! That hat looks like a pimple on an elephant. Go and put it on properly.'

Marie told me that another memory of her training was the long hours they worked with only one day off a week. During training at Bideford Hospital they did 11 nights on night duty and then two off, followed by another 11 nights on. But they did get their dinner in the Board Room, served by Matron! Staff were not allowed off duty on Christmas Day between 7.30a.m. and 9.30p.m. The doctors carved the turkey and the nurses made their day part of the ward's Christmas. When Marie became a ward sister her family also spent their Christmas with the patients on the ward. Her nursing interest overlapped into her spare time as she was a member of the St John Ambulance Brigade. When she retired as Area Commissioner she had served 37 years with the Brigade and had been made a Commander of the Order of St John.

You can always rely on some funny stories from a hospital porter and one such is Len Shaddick, who worked at the NDI many years ago. He told me about a nurse who was afraid to move around the corridors of the hospital at night as she had been told of a ghost in the operating theatre. She would phone the porter's lodge and ask for an

School nurse Peggy Bate (now Langdon) who enjoyed archery in her spare time.

escort through the theatre. Len was on night duty and was called to remove a deceased patient from a ward with this nurse. This meant bringing the body down in the lift and wheeling it out across the yard to the mortuary over some uneven humps in the tarmac. When they went over one of the bumps there was a clattering noise but as it was dark they could not see what had caused it. On the way back one of them tripped on something. It turned out to be a set of false teeth – the answer to the clatter on the way to the mortuary! Len and his companion then had to retrace their steps and repeat all the procedures to reunite the dentures with their late owner!

In this chapter on the medical health of the town we cannot forget the school nurse. Peggy Langdon, who would probably be better remembered as Mrs Bate, held the post for 18 years, covering Barnstaple, Braunton, Ilfracombe, Bratton Fleming, Lynton and Parracombe, responsible for the care of approximately 3,000 children. Peggy, who originates from South Molton, spent the war years nursing in different London hospitals. When she returned to Devon and married Edgar Bate she worked in the maternity ward at the NDI. When her own children were older she returned to nursing. She told me of one of her visits to a school where she found a young lad with head lice and sent him home with a letter for his mother, asking her to come to the school clinic on the next day. The mother did not arrive so Peggy asked the boy if he had given his mother the note. 'Oh yes, Miss,' he replied, 'but she said you were an old cow.' 'Did she indeed,' said Peggy, 'but I'm not, am I?' 'No Miss, 'cos a cow's got four legs!'

Chapter Twelve

EMERGENCY SERVICES

Barnstaple's Fire Brigade in the early-twentieth century. This photograph may have been taken at the Country Station at the bottom of Sticklepath.

Most of us take our emergency services for granted until we are in need of their aid. It is only then that we really appreciate their skill and professionalism. When you realise that a few generations ago there was no such luxury as the '999' service you wonder how the townspeople managed when a fire broke out or when there was a medical emergency.

The Fire Service

In the early part of the last century Barnstaple had two fire stations – the Country Station on the Sticklepath side of the bridge at Shapland and Petters, and the

The firemen dining 'al fresco' while camping at Combe Martin when an oil pipeline was laid from Wales in 1939.

Town Station at the back of Queen Anne's Walk by Castle Quay (this was demolished in 1976 and at the time of writing is a walled garden).

Harold Mock, who was born in 1911 in Congrams Close, Newport, joined the Auxiliary Fire Service in 1939 and became a full-time fireman with the Devon County Fire Service. This was a time of war and Harold not only worked in Barnstaple where he attended a fire at the British Restaurant, but was also sent to Southampton and Plymouth when these cities were being blitzed. Harold recalls being on standby near Combe Martin when a pipeline was laid across the Bristol

127

Fire Service

Left: *The Borough Police Force and Fire Brigade on parade on the Square, c.1910.*

Lady Peto christening a new fire engine (possibly the first motorised vehicle), c.1925.

Right: *Firemen testing new equipment near the Town Station, c.1940. Left to right: ?, ?, Hutchings, Gale, ?, Smalldon, Thomas Parsley, ?.*

Fire crew at the Fire Station opposite Padfields, 1959.
Left to right: *Freddy Parkin, ?, ?, ?, ? Ashton, Fred Offield, George Kettle, Arthur Hill, ?, Jimmy Cottle, ?;* **seated:** *Leading Fireman Harold Mock, ?, Station Officer Bill Heywood, George Ashton.*

Channel to carry petroleum oil. As the oil is inflammable the firemen had to camp out on the hillside in shifts, lasting several days at a time.

The Fire Brigade moved to Boutport Street opposite Padfields Shop in 1935, but this was very cramped. The town finally got a purpose-built station in 1965 at the bottom of North Road (known as New Road) and Harold became a Sub-Divisional Officer there.

The Police Force

In 1836 a pensioner by the name of Cousins was made the first town constable and with the help of two Beadles attempted to bring law and order to Barnstaple – an almost impossible task in a town with more than 80 public houses! The Town Council's Watch Committee took on another three night-watchmen. The constable (who was to be constantly on duty!) was paid ten shillings a week and the night-watchmen eight shillings in summer and ten shillings during the winter. They were supplied with great-coats, staves, rattles and lanterns. Soon afterwards the Watch Committee appointed John Evans, a bookseller who lived in the Cattle Market, as a superintendent with an onerous job description. He had to be:

... constantly on alert and perambulating the streets during the day; attend the police office until 2 o' clock every morning to direct the proceedings of the night police; and be active on market days in regulating the markets and the disposition of carts.

Mr Evans did not stay long in the job.

The Town Council finally had to face the fact that Barnstaple was rife with drunkenness and debauchery. The Mayor requested help from the Home Secretary, who sent an undercover officer to root out the problem. This plan came to a sudden halt when the officer concerned was waylaid and viciously attacked on Long Bridge, which cost the Council £7 for medical treatment and compensation.

Prisons and punishments in the town before the twentieth century were probably no better or worse than any other town in the country, but when reading accounts of them I feel the penal system left a lot to be desired. There was a prison on the Square where convicts were kept in a filthy hole and viewed by the public through a grating. There was also a lock-up beside the Quay Hall next to Cross Street and it was common practice for the populace to poke fun as well as sticks through the bars at the unfortunate inmates. Further along the Quay was another instrument of humiliation – a wooden cage where drunks and disorderly people or noisy young boys spent a few hours until they had come to their senses or sobered up.

When the Borough Constabulary amalgamated with the Devon Force in 1921 the Police Station, which had been at the Guildhall, transferred to the old prison building in Castle Street. Keith James was a probationary police constable in Barnstaple in 1954/5 and remembers the Police Station well. He said the prison part of the building was a very cold and uninviting place with whitewashed walls. When he returned in the 1960s this part of the station was only used as a storage area. It was demolished in 1977 and is now the car park belonging to the Probation Office (now named Kingsley House).

In Keith's early days in the force in the 1950s he recalls that his weekly pay was £9.5s.3d., which included a boot allowance. He can also remember the Chief Constable Lt Col Rudolf Ranulf Monsell Bacon (known as 'Rasher Bacon') who was proud that he knew the names of all 460 policemen in the Devon Force.

On his return to Barnstaple in 1963 Keith and his wife Clarice were allocated a police house in Charles Street. The couple laugh when they recall that the house had an outside loo and just before they moved in it was agreed to build a bathroom and inside toilet for them. On moving-in day they arrived with all their goods and chattels to find the dining-room filled with a huge pile of sand and were told by the builders that they weren't expected until the following week.

Keith was a motor patrol man for the next 13 years, sometimes doing a 12-hour shift around an area from Bideford Quay to the Portsmouth Arms on the A377 and out as far as Swimbridge. Keith reminisces about the fair when it was held on North Walk and the road was closed to traffic between Queen Anne's Walk and Mermaid Cross. His other memories of the fair are of the crowds that used to gather outside the Guildhall when the fair proclamation was read and the white-gloved hand of welcome was displayed; and the spiced ale made to a secret recipe that caused one sergeant to fall asleep at his desk after sampling the brew.

The Police Station had to remain open 24 hours of the day and Keith remembers the food stalls outside the charge-room window and the smell of hotdogs wafting through into the station. He also recalls the stall-holders who would plug their equipment into the electricity supply in the police house in Castle Street to illuminate their stalls, giving the policeman a basket of fruit as a 'thank you' at the end of their stay.

When traffic flowed both ways in High Street, cars were permitted to park on one side one day and on the other side the next. It meant that the waiting-restriction signs had to be changed overnight. This entailed the night-duty policeman having to walk the streets adjusting every sign. With the aid of his truncheon the 'bobbie' would either release the catch at the top of the roundel to let down the metal half-circle, or push it up to secure it at the top. Keith says that great care had to taken not to let the flap drop and make a clatter or you would see all the lights go on in the bedrooms nearby.

Keith served in Barnstaple from 1963 until he retired in 1989, except for a one-day posting to Bideford which lasted 16 months! He stayed on at Barnstaple Police Station as a civilian Coroner's Officer, finally retiring in 2000.

Devon Constabulary, 1903. Only two policemen are from Barnstaple.

DEVON CONSTABULARY, A Division, May, 1903.

Below: *Barnstaple Divison of Devon Constabulary on Castle Green, late 1950s. Left to right, back row: ?, ?, ?, ?, PC Ken Whitfield, ?, D. Tamplin, DC Sam Griffiths, PC W. Lewis, MPCs Charlie Taylor, Arthur Chapple, Dave Janes and George Mead; third row: Sgt Osborne, PC Arthur Williams, PC Mike Jardine, PC Terry Shirtridge, PC Terry Gay, ?, PC Don Hill, ?, ?, ?, ?, ?, ?, ?, ?, Sgt Len Ellis; second row: ?, ?, PC Pat Connolly, PC Reg Long, PC Bill Bush, ?, ?, PC Norman Brooks, PC Peter Plant, ?, ?, ?, ?, PC Adrian Addwell; front row: D/Sgt Reg Fear, ?, Sgt Mike Coleman, Sgt George Spry, ?, D/Insp. Ron Ferris, Ch/Insp. Charlie Parsons, Supt Jewell, H.W. Kempton, Insp. Bill Bond, Sgt Ron Honeywell, ?, ?, Sgt W.D. Stocker.*

✌ Policing the Town ⯈

Barnstaple Police in the fair procession along the Strand, c.1960. PC Bill Lewis (now Revd Lewis) is at the rear of the group on the left. Pictured front left is Sgt Len Lewis, with PC Norman Brooks (back right) and Sgt George Spry (front right). Chief Inspector Bicknell leads the parade.

The first time white lines were painted on Long Bridge warranted this photograph to be taken. The taxi at the front was driven by Ernie Webber of Silver Street. (In 2002 the Square this devoid of traffic would certainly be a rarity!) Photograph R.L. Knight.

Left: *Chief Supt Reg Goldsworthy presents Chief Insp. John Edwards of Barnstaple with the Police Medal for Bravery for saving the life of a drowning man at Bideford. Others in the group are, left to right: Supt Brian Phillips, DCI Bayliss, Chief Insp. Graham Morrish and Insp. Stan Dibble.*

Three new ambulances for the St John Ambulance Brigade outside Bale's Garage on the Square, 1951.

during the Lynmouth flood disaster in 1952. In 1963 he became the Chief Controller of the Ambulance Service in North Devon and from 1974 until his retirement in 1980 he held the post of Divisional Commander.

The Ambulance Service

The Ambulance Service as we know it is relatively new compared to the other two major emergency services. Up to 1946 the St John Ambulance Brigade was responsible for the ambulance that answered your 999 call.

One ambulanceman, who worked for both the original brigade and the present-day Westcountry Ambulance Service, is Michael Balman who told me about some of his experiences in the job. In the mid 1960s Michael became a full-time ambulanceman when Devon County Council paid them for their daytime work. However, St John still carried on the night-time and also weekend cover voluntarily. When Michael and his wife Marie lived in King Edward Street he took his ambulance home in case he was called out at night. One morning he realised he'd forgotten to lock the ambulance doors when he found a tramp asleep in the back of the vehicle!

Dick and Rene Braddon.

Although Michael says that much of his time was spent accompanying patients to hospitals he also played the role of midwife on three occasions, delivering one baby in the ambulance, one in a caravan and another at home. Michael's career with the St John Ambulance Brigade spans more than 42 years. He has been the Area Staff Officer for the Cadets and is now the Area Vice President for North Devon. He is also an Officer of the Order of St John.

Dick Braddon first became interested in St John during the Second World War when he worked at Shapland and Petter and took a first-aid class. In 1946 he was persuaded to take on the post of Superintendent with the Brigade when Fred Knott wanted to retire. Dick and his wife Rene lived in Richmond Street and Rene manned the telephone system. When an ambulance was required she took the call at home and then passed on the message to the drivers at the ambulance station in Commercial Road. In 1950 Dick and Rene moved to the flat over the ambulance station, which proved helpful one night when Dick was taking his turn on ambulance duty. Rene told me that maternity cases were taken to either Grenville Nursing Home at Bideford or Bicclescombe Park Nursing Home in Ilfracombe. Dick was in the ambulance taking an expectant mother to Bideford when Rene received another urgent call to take a maternity case to Ilfracombe. Rene gauged the time that Dick's ambulance would be travelling down Sticklepath Hill and, as she knew he would be able to see their flat from there, she switched the bedroom light on and off. Dick saw the light flashing and realised Rene was trying to contact him. He stopped off and collected his further instructions – not exactly hi-tech communications, but effective nonetheless!

Dick and Rene Braddon have both worked for many years for the benefit of the St John Ambulance Brigade in Barnstaple and Dick is a Knight of the Order of St John. In 2000 Princess Margaret opened the Brigade's new premises in Princess Street. It is named after Dick – Braddon House.

SHOWTIME

Chapter Thirteen

The Girls' Life Brigade hold their Queen of Queens pageant in the Foresters' Hall, 1948. The Queen was Celia Aze and Miss Ayre is the lady in uniform. Sitting on the left is Diane Bosence and on the right is Jennifer Garnish.

John Gay was without doubt Barnstaple's best-known dramatist and following in his footsteps through the years the town has shown a great deal of interest and talent on the theatrical scene. There have been several theatres in the town in the past 200 years. Theatre Lane, which leads from the Strand to the High Street, is aptly named as there was once a theatre here, behind the Angel Hotel. When it closed a group of people got together, formed a company and built a new theatre in Boutport Street. It was opened in 1833 and was at first named the Grecian Theatre and later renamed the Theatre Royal. In 1893 after a period of disuse it was refurbished by the Bridge Trust, making it one of the best-equipped theatres in the area. The building was eventually demolished and rebuilt as the Gaumont Cinema in 1931.

The John Gay Theatre was built in 1937 from a converted cabinet works at the bottom of Newport where cars for sale are displayed at the time of writing. The John Gay Players were a repertory company who staged plays here and at other times concert parties held shows in the small theatre. When it closed in 1950 the company moved to the Foresters' Hall in High Street. This large hall was owned by the Loyal Order of Foresters and it was here that many shows and dances were held up until the 1950s. Sheila Gear's uncle was the secretary of the Foresters and Sheila remembers playing on the stage with her friend and pretending they were famous actresses.

In the twenty-first century the Queen's Theatre in Boutport Street has had many famous artists on its programmes, but I wonder if they realise that in 1850 the stage was in a room on the top floor over the Corn Market! The Albert Hall, as it was called originally – after Queen Victoria's consort – hosted many theatrical productions, cinema shows and dances, with the added attraction of an organ that came up from the orchestra pit. This came to an

133

❧ Barnstaple's Theatres ❧

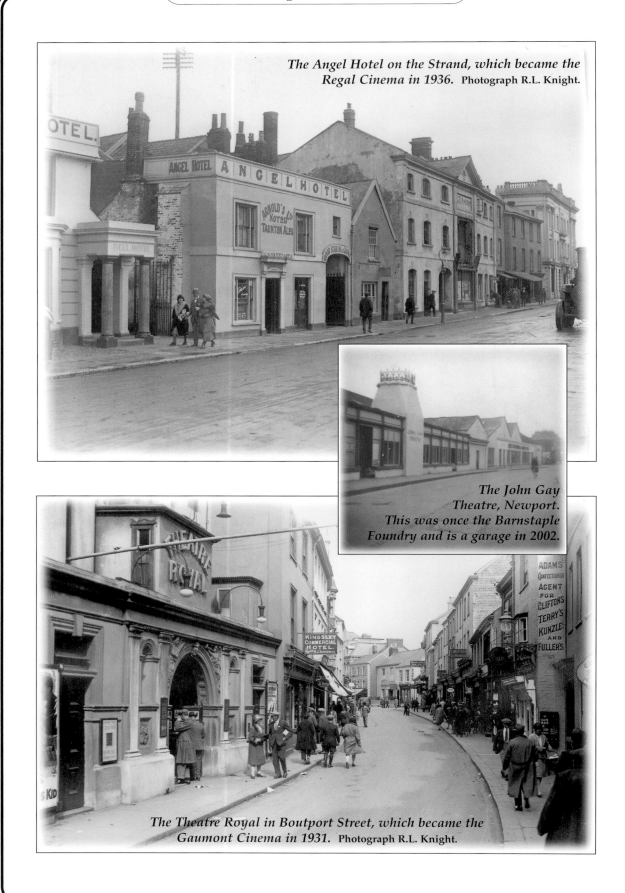

The Angel Hotel on the Strand, which became the Regal Cinema in 1936. Photograph R.L. Knight.

The John Gay Theatre, Newport. This was once the Barnstaple Foundry and is a garage in 2002.

The Theatre Royal in Boutport Street, which became the Gaumont Cinema in 1931. Photograph R.L. Knight.

❧ Dramatic Productions ❧

Right: *Members of the Musical Comedy Society in* The Pyjama Game, *1959. Pictured at the back are Diane Bosence and Sandra Dayman. Left to right, front row: Bob Aston, Alec Thorne, Pat Tucker, Jill Hatton, Pearl Purchase.* Photograph by kind permission of the *Western Morning News*.

Left: *A Musical Comedy Society production of* South Pacific *in 1966. On the ladder is Peter Oke, with Grace Molland standing. Left to right, back row: Diane Newcombe, ?, Joan Dyke, Shirley Crocker, Gillian Squire, Patricia Ennion, Valerie Turvey, Violet Windsor, Julie Shute; front row: Jane Bryant, June Morgan, Elizabeth Foot, Jean Blake, Janet Bolt, Diane Bosence, Mary Hill, Patricia Burrington, Janet Couldrake, Janet Smale.*

Right: *Barnstaple Amateur Operatic Society in their 100th anniversary production of* Iolanthe. *Left to right: Alan Stewart, Steve Chamberlain, Carole Blight, Tony Freeman, Malcolm Bowen, John Carvosso.*

Left: *John Huxtable, Pat Cole and Bill Courtney in the 1963 production of* Vagabond King.

end in 1941 when the building burnt down. It was eventually rebuilt in 1952 and renamed the Queen's Hall to celebrate the new reign of Queen Elizabeth II.

Over the years the theatre has been the hub of North Devon's professional and amateur dramatic art with many shows, plays and bands taking to the boards. It is here also that parliamentary successes have been declared and celebrated, where carnival queens have been chosen and civic and social banquets and dances held. A few of the many local groups and organisations which have delighted the North Devon people and graced the Barnstaple stage over the past century are: the Operatic Society, the Musical Comedy Society and Esme Preston's Dancing School.

Flossie Shapland first joined the Musical Comedy Society in 1920 when she was 13. She told me that the society started in Pilton Church Hall and her first show was *Sherwood's Queen*. The venue changed to the Theatre Royal in Boutport Street where Mrs Killard-Levy helped stage the early productions such as *The Dogs of Devon*, *The Country Girl*, *The Arcadians*, *Miss Hook of Holland* and *The Quaker Girl*.

Barnstaple Operatic Society was formed in 1900 and members celebrated their 100th anniversary by staging Gilbert and Sullivan's *Iolanthe*, which had also been their very first performance. Peggy and John Huxtable are life members of the society and Peggy tells me that she joined in 1925 when they staged *The Gondoliers*. At first, productions were staged in the Theatre Royal, but during the First World War the society cancelled their shows. In 1920 Peggy's dentist father, Garfield Pearce, and solicitor John Brewer reopened the society. When the Theatre Royal closed the company moved to the Albert Hall, but after the fire in 1941 other venues had to be found, such as the John Gay Theatre and even the Regal Cinema. Peggy told me that the cinema did not have dressing rooms so the cast had to use rooms in the Bell Hotel next door. There was much confusion and fun as they dashed between buildings to change costumes for the different scenes!

Miss Esme Preston.

An early poster of an Esme Preston show held in the Foresters' Hall.

There is a friendly rivalry between the Musical Comedy and Operatic Societies and both spend many hours each year rehearsing their week-long stage productions, which could put many professional companies to shame. These performances are held in the Queen's Theatre and rarely are there any empty seats in the auditorium. Charities benefit from the profits made.

Many of the dancers who take part in the societies' shows have been pupils of the legendary dance teacher Miss Esme Preston. I can write with some authority as I was taught ballet, American tap, musical comedy and acrobatic dancing from four years of age until I left to get married, by which time I had become one of her assistants. A Liverpudlian, she came to Ilfracombe via Wales where she had married Charles Paxford. Miss Preston was a stickler for good manners so no one called her Esme – well, not to her face anyway! Before arriving in Ilfracombe in 1927 she had a dance school in Aberdare and once she had settled in North Devon she decided to restart her teaching career. She obtained a £60 loan from her friendly bank manager, Mr Cross, which was to be repaid at 1s. a week. When he enquired about the name of this new school she admitted that she had not decided. Mr Cross suggested that as she lived in Portland Street it should be the Portland Dance Academy. I clearly remember our black tunics with the gold embroidered letters PDA on the left shoulder. During the Second World War Miss Preston not only continued with her yearly show but also put on shows for the troops. Costumes were made out of remnants (quite often blackout material) and remodelled for other shows. In 1941 the programme said:

Dress materials and costumes are rationed – Nearly all the male members of the Troupe are in the Forces – The blackout continues, but in spite of all the obstacles, 'The Show Goes On'!

In her book of the same title Miss Preston's daughter Sandra wrote that she was only four years old when she joined the concert parties. She remembers singing

Left: *Jill Ford, a talented acrobatic pupil, who stunned audiences with her flexible contortions.*

Right: *Barnstaple's senior pupils in the Summer Show, 1961/2.* Left to right: *Avril Barthram, Jackie Halfpenny, Susan Stewart, Daphne Walton, Jane Goodliffe, Jane Toogood;* sitting: *Marlene Miller, Pauline Fogwell, Elaine Norris.*

to the American troops; 'Got any gum chum?', to which they replied by throwing packets of chewing gum to her on the stage.

In 1947 Miss Preston brought her shows to Barnstaple and at about the same time started giving lessons in the town. In those days she did not drive so had to travel by bus from Ilfracombe carrying cases and bags of shoes, music, books and always a very large handbag, which resembled a bottomless pit. Lessons commenced at 9a.m. which meant you had to be ready at the barre smartly turned-out with your hair up and ready for *'pliés* in first position'. My memories of these Saturday dance lessons are of the hard physical work, the tired legs, the sweat running down my face and my toes bleeding from block shoes. But there was also euphoria when I achieved a step or movement which brought praise from my teacher. Other memories are of shafts of sunlight glinting through the windows onto the dust rising off the wooden floors from the stomping of our tap

shoes. And of boys outside hanging onto the window ledges and peering in to see what went on in the mystical world of little girls prancing about in short tunics. The usual call was 'Gaw'on, show us yer knickers!'

Those of us who were Miss Preston's pupils will know what it was like to be on the end of her quick temper and piercing blue eyes. She accepted nothing but your best efforts and we respected and appreciated her knowledge, encouragement, discipline and professionalism. Her success can only be quantified by the number of pupils she taught in 52 years in North Devon. Many went on to join famous ballet companies and others to take up professional careers in the entertainment world. Miss Preston had two aims – to achieve perfection in her pupils' exam results and to show this talent to the people of North Devon. Her first pantomime was in Ilfracombe in 1944 and before long she was also staging a summer show in Barnstaple.

The company of Esme Preston's 1956 Barnstaple Summer Show. Left to right, back row: ?, Pauline Badcock, Avril Brodie, Pamela Cullen, Yvonne ?, Sandra Paxford, Elaine Burton, Diana Battrick, Penny Goodridge, Ann Bament, Pauline Lane, Diane Barrow, Pat Sanderson; fourth row: Janet Stevens, Anne Kyatt, Jill Ford, Sandra Kay, Elaine Norris, Joyce Trott; third row includes: Rosemary King, Jane Toogood, Eleanor Peters, Janet Couldrake, ?, Janet Gayton, Susan Bate, ?,

Alison Bate, Angela Legg, ?, Cynthia Smith, Gillian Perryman, Jackie Halfpenny, Suzanne Cutliffe; second row: ?, Avril Barthram, Sandra Dayman, Jackie Thorburn, Jane Chapman, Jennifer ?, Pat Robins, Michael Barrow, Diane Thorne, ?, Ann Dymond, ?, Pat Spiegelhalter, Janet Fry, Ann Knill; front row: Marlene Miller, Rosemary Isaac, Ann Miller, Jennifer Trick, Janet Norman, ?, Sally Manley, Gillian Beer, Deidrie Raine, Pauline Fogwell.

137

Left: *William Gee, the first Commissionaire at the Gaumont Cinema.*

Right: *George Wilks on the left after winning an Al Jolson talent competition. The manager, Ian Carpenter, is at the back of the group.*

Above: *Staff at the Gaumont Cinema in the 1930s. Left to right, back row: Miss Gooding, William Gee, Lawrie Mitchell, ?, Miss Cooper (cashier), Mr Potter, Mrs Dark, Charlie Lake, ?, Mr Cutler, ?; front row: ?, ?, Miss French, Miss Guilliam, Miss Morris, Manager Mr Carpenter, Miss Balment, ?, Miss Featherstone, the other names are unknown.*

These shows entailed a tremendous amount of organisation, which was another of Miss Preston's talents. Her daughter Sandra Paxford wrote the scripts for the shows but the songs, dances and scenery were arranged and choreographed by Miss Preston. She designed the costumes, went to London to choose and buy the material, and then persuaded the mothers to make the clothes. One year I was definitely in my mother's bad books when I volunteered her to make 14 costumes for one dance routine! The booking of the theatres, the sale of the tickets, the press releases, the lighting and the make-up were all attended to personally by this formidable lady. During the show she was always to be found in the wings, intent on every word spoken or sung and every toe pointed. An apron round her waist with a huge pocket contained every article required for last-minute repairs – hairbrush, make-up, safety pins, hair grips and, of course, the script. With silent authority she would organise entry and exits on the stage at the same time as loudly whispering directions to the lighting man, those working the curtains and the scene-shifters. No one, but no one, answered back. Her husband Charlie, a watch and jewellery repairer, dedicated his spare time to helping his wife in her show-business life. He built and painted all the scenery. He was a quiet man and you were aware of Miss Preston's mood when you heard her yell 'Charlie!', followed by a complaint about a piece of scenery or a prop that was missing.

She always told us that a disastrous dress-rehearsal was good (and many went on late with parents waiting at the stage door to collect their charges) as it would be all right on the night! All the hard work usually culminated in a first-class evening of dancing, singing and comedy from which many charities benefited. There were only two occasions when the shows did not go on (but were only postponed). The first time was in 1960 when Miss Preston was diag-nosed with cancer and only given a short while to live, unless she had immediate surgery and treatment. The second time was in the big freeze of 1963.

On 2 November 1982 the footlights suddenly went out and the show came to an end for Esme Preston. The shock at the news of her death was shared by all who had experienced her talent for over half a century. Most said, 'I thought she would go on for ever.'

In the early part of the 1900s cinemas were a popular part of the town's entertainment. In 1919 the Foresters' Hall in Bear Street was billed as an up-to-date picture house and the Palace Cinema in Silver Street was called the Cozy Kinema, where Mr Trengrove was the pianist. The Theatre Royal and the Albert Hall also featured the latest heartthrobs of the silver screen.

In the 1930s two new cinemas were built – the Gaumont in Boutport Street and the Regal on the Strand. Keith James remembers his granny paying for him to go to the Saturday morning pictures for 6d. at the Gaumont and how the manager, Ian Carpenter, whom the children called Uncle Mac, would get them to sing before the entertainment began: 'Come along on Saturday mornings, Greeting everyone with a smile.' Keith told me that when it was your birthday you received a card and could take a friend in for free.

Eric Bennett remembers that the cinemas were very strict when it came to allowing minors in to see category 'A' (for adults) films. If he wanted to see one of these films he would have to wait around outside hoping someone over the age of 14 would take responsibility for him. Quite often this meant a long fruitless wait and he would have to go home after the last picture had started and try again the next night.

When the film *The Jolson Story* was screened at the Gaumont the manager held a talent competition every night for the best singer of a Jolson song. Sheila Wilks remembers her father George sang the 'Anniversary Song' and came second at the end of the week.

Chapter Fourteen

HOBBIES, INTERESTS & SPORTS

Pigeon fancying was once classed as a poor man's sport and associated with cloth-capped men from northern mill towns. But of course this is not the case. There are many rich and famous people who are hooked on this sport, including the Queen who has her own loft at Sandringham. In Barnstaple it was a major interest for many years and although there are not so many enthusiasts in the town today it still exists.

Arthur Squires told me that he used to race pigeons and although he is still keen he had to give it up when the cost of sending his birds away to race became too expensive. Arthur explained his method of training. He would take the young birds in a basket to Barnstaple Station, where they would be put on the train with a note for the stationmaster at the Portsmouth Arms or Eggesford saying, 'Please release the birds at (stating a time) weather permitting.' The stationmaster would record the time he let the birds go and Arthur, who was waiting patiently for their return to the loft, could then

work out how long it had taken them to get home.

Roger Andrews told me that there used to be four clubs in the town – Barnstaple Continental Flying Club, North Devon Premier Club, Barnstaple Racing Pigeon Society and Pilton Invitation Flying Club. The last two are still in existence at the time of writing.

Roger has many memories of his childhood and pigeon-racing antics in the Pottington area. His grandfather raced birds and then Roger and his brother Peter (Archie) became interested in the sport. They had a cock and hen which they had caught while the birds were feeding on Rolle Quay. The cock bird was a Silver Mealy which Roger kept and Peter had the bronze hen. The boys took the birds to Taunton and released them to see what their time was like on the home run. The cock came back but the hen is still away with the birds!

Roger described a race day at Pottington. The pigeons would be sent away and released at the given time while the folk at home waited by their lofts for the first birds to return. Once inside the loft the rubber ring

Fred Offield outside his pigeon loft in Rolle Street.

would have to be taken off a bird's leg. One of the lads then ran with the ring to the club stewards where it was 'clocked in'. Roger says his mother told him that when she was young and her father's pigeons came home from a race she and two school friends would cut down on the time by running in relay from Pottington to Rolle Quay Inn, where the clock was kept.

In the 1960s and '70s Tippler racing was very popular in Barnstaple. This is where a flock called a 'kit' of birds flies around in a circle for more than eight but less than 24 hours. If one bird drops out of the flying the whole kit is disqualified. The longest-flying kit is the winner. Roger has childhood memories of sitting at Fairview for hours, watching the birds flying round and round.

Another form of bird fancying was shown to me by Arthur Roulestone at the 112th annual show of the Barnstaple and District Caged Bird Society held at Park School in 2001. Here I found rows of birds in a magnificent array of colours. Arthur has been a member of the society for 75 years and a birdman since before he can remember. His brother Robert is also a lifelong member. The fascination for these beautiful small birds was inherited from their father

Arthur, grandfather Fred and great-grandfather John, who all specialised in British birds.

The first bird show Arthur can recall was at the Foresters' Hall in the High Street. He also remembers the caged-bird shows in the Pannier Market, which were popular three-day events with Marine bands and other attractions. This show was not just for small birds but chickens, ducks, rabbits and almost anything that would fit into a cage!

Arthur said the largest show was held at West Regional Autos (later Cox's Garage) at the bottom of Newport and attracted around 1,000 entrants. Before and after the Second World War birds were brought from as far as Yorkshire for a show. Arthur would go over to the railway station with a hand-cart during the night, collect the cages with the birds and take them to the Foresters' Hall, then set them out on tables and feed, water and settle them for the next day.

Many silver trophies were awarded on the day I attended the show and Arthur explained that when Charles Dart, who was a keen bird fancier and breeder, was the mayor he instigated silver trophies to be presented by the town councillors to the society.

Left: *Pigeon fanciers: Pilton Invitation Flying Club, c.1980. Left to right, back row:* Arthur Hill, Peter Mock, Bobby Hill, Bobby Bates, ?, Charlie Kemp (Sec.); *seated:* ?, ?, Jimmy Cottle, ?, Fred Offield, Bob Seymour.

A pigeon carrier releasing the birds at the start of a race.

❧ Caged Bird Society ❧

Barnstaple Caged Bird Society Competition, 1930. Sitting in the front to the right is Jack Miller.

Arthur Roulestone is pictured on the right with his brother Robert at the 112th Barnstaple and District Caged Bird Society Show in 2001.

✥ Bowls ✥

Another of Alderman Dart's interests was the game of bowls. He was a member of the Newport Club and on 17 June 1935 he opened their new club at Rock Park. Previously the club had been based at the top of Newport and met in the public house. In 1952 the club was renamed Rock Park Bowling Club, but it was not until 1998 that ladies were allowed to join the playing ranks. Eric (Breezy) Bennett has been the secretary and treasurer for almost 40 years.

Newport and Victoria Bowling Club, 1901.

Left and below: *A game of bowls, c.1920.*

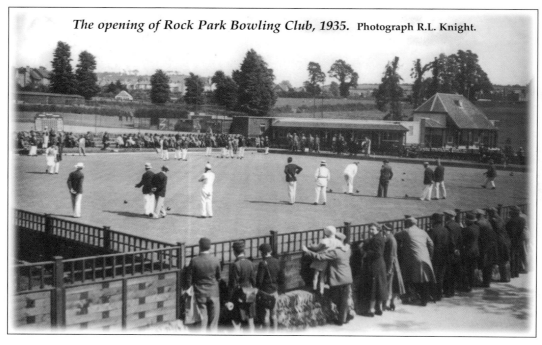

The opening of Rock Park Bowling Club, 1935. Photograph R.L. Knight.

✑ Bowls ✑

Left: Eric Bennett first bowled at the Rock Park Club in 1962 and became the secretary and treasurer the year after, and still holds these posts in 2002. In 1998 Eric was made a life member of the Devon County Bowling Association for his contribution to the sport.

Below: *United Services Bowling Club in the 1960s. Those standing include: Arthur Lyddon, Jack Spry, Bill Cooper, Norman Duckett, Mrs Phillips, Archie Thorne, ?, ?, ?, ?; centre: Ken Reilly, Frank Clarke, Tom Mogridge, Dai Hartnoll, Harry Hopper, Hilda Dix, Mrs Knott, ?, Freddie Parkin; with, left to right, kneeling: Mrs Hutchings, ?, Nancy Hopper, Mrs Evans, Wynn Reilly.*

Rock Park Bowling Club Presidents Day, 1966. Left to right, back row: J. Furseman, F. Lane, E. Bennett, C. Wakely, W. Gill, Ald. F. Dunning, J. Bush, E. Loudwill, W. Symons, R. Miller, M. Symons, W. Willis; centre: F. Harding, A. Davies, R. Bailey, C. Dymond, A. Penfold, F. Downing, A. Cann, W. Stocker; front row: J. Searle, G. Reed, C. Webber, J. Ball, D. Evans (President), C. Lancey, J. Hennessey, G. Courtnay, L. Higgins.

❧ *Poolside Fun* ❧

Barnstaple Swimming Club water polo team 1936/37/38. Left to right, back row: B. Ansell, G. Buscombe, J. Featherstone, P. Hill; front row: W. Stone, G. Summers, D. Brooks.

Below: Joan Webber and Marion Brown teaching girls at the pool in 1948.

Barnstaple youngsters enjoying the open-air pool.

Swimming

Before the first municipal swimming baths were opened in Rock Park in May 1932, the children learnt to swim either in the Rivers Taw and Yeo or at the nearest beaches. These new open-air baths, which cost £6,076.16s.3d. to build, were a welcome addition to the town amenities and very much appreciated. Also in 1932, Barnstaple Swimming Club was formed at a meeting in the Guildhall, where the Mayor Bruce Oliver recalled an unofficial 'club' in 1897 which daringly used the iron bridge that took trains across the river from the Junction Station.

The new baths soon had a programme of swimming, diving and life saving. Galas and water polo matches were also arranged. Schoolchildren were taken to the pool for lessons once a week and I have clear memories of hot summer days when we walked from the Girls' Secondary Modern School in Ashleigh Road for our weekly lesson. The brilliant white walls and seats glowed against sparkling water, which took on the azure look of a Mediterranean paradise from the blue-painted pool walls. Sometimes the water was freezing, but it was also exhilarating.

Photographer Tony Freeman was a keen club member and he recalls the Rock Park training sessions when the water at the start of the season in April was rarely above 40°F and at best never above 70°F. He was in both the junior and senior water polo teams and on occasions represented the county in competitions. In one year they achieved a unique double by winning two major titles.

Peter Hill, who celebrated the Swimming Club's 70th anniversary in 2002, has been a member since that first meeting. He retired from the post of president and is now a patron. It is interesting to note that past presidents of the club include Mr Heppenstall, the headmaster who used to take the boys down to the Taw to teach them to swim, and Mr Critchley who was the senior master at the grammar school.

Barnstaple's prize-winning water polo team, 1970. This was the first time in the history of Barnstaple Swimming Club that the senior team won the Devon First Division League and the Devon Senior Knockout Cup in the same season. Left to right: Tony Freeman, Bill Braily, Clive Symons, Dave Gaydon, George Wingfield, Peter Melmouth, John Balman (Captain), Mike Davey (Goalkeeper), Ray Malborough, Len Essary.

Three competitors at an early gala held by the Swimming Club in 1933. Left to right: Jimmy Hill, Cyril Webber, Lewis Jeffery.

North Devon Dolphins, the under-18s water polo team, in 1983. The team had several triumphs in this year. Left to right, back row: Cyril Webber (Coach), D. Lavalette, N. Smith, A. Brown, S. Smale, A. Cottenham, K. Smale; front row: C. Hodges, S. Watts, M. Slee, A. Miles, A. Watts.

Other keen supporters of the Swimming Club were Dougie and Rosie Potter and Joan and Cyril Webber. Cyril died in 1998 and Joan told me about his swimming career. He was a fine swimmer, although his first love was cycle racing. During the Second World War, when Cyril served with the RAF in the Middle East, he formed a water polo team and once took on a challenge from King Farouk's bodyguards. He went to Australia as an Olympic trialist. He coached the North Devon Dolphins and the Devon water polo team and ran courses at Crystal Palace. He had successes in Malta, Italy, Australia and in New Zealand, where he became a legend when coaching their national water polo team for the World Games in California. He went on to become the Australian team manager. Cyril Webber spearheaded fund-raising for the hydrotherapy pool at North Devon District Hospital and was a prime mover in raising funds to build the present Leisure Centre. Joan said Cyril had great pleasure when this was opened as he remembered only too well that when he was aiming for the Olympics all those years before he had nowhere locally to train.

❧ *Swimming Winners* ❧

Devon champions in the late 1940s.
Left to right: *Ray Furseman, Keith Seymour, Cyril Webber, Jack Turvey.*

Motor Club

Born at Snapper near Goodleigh in 1918, Bob Ray worked on his parents' farm but joined the Army in time for his 21st birthday and the start of the Second World War. He became an instructor in the Motor Transport Wing, training the Commandos to ride their motorcycles over rough terrain. After the war he rode professionally for the Aerial Motor Cycle factory in Birmingham. He told me it was usual for him to ride over 40,000 miles a year.

In 1946 he started his first motorcycle business in a lock-up shop in Braunton and many people will remember his shops and garages in Barnstaple and Newport. In the same year, Bob and his pals Bob Harris and Ron Woolaway founded the North Devon Motor Club. They formed a group of motorcycle and motor-car enthusiasts and from the club's headquarters at the New Inn at Muddiford they arranged rallies, scrambles and trials where they could pit their skills riding over hills and hazardous country or racing on circuits.

In 1948 in San Remo, Bob began a ten-year career with the International Motorcycle Team, competing in countries such as Holland, Belgium, Italy, France, Czechoslovakia and Russia as well as the United Kingdom. Between 1949 and 1955 Bob's Aerial Team won many first prizes and are still the proud holders of eight gold medals. Bob retired from the business in 1986 and spent the following years enjoying yachting in and around Spain. He has now returned to his native Barnstaple. The North Devon Motor Club is still going strong and in 2000 was awarded the title of the Best Motor Club in the British Isles.

Above: *The Barnstaple and District Motorcycle and Light Car Club line up outside the Athenaeum in the 1920s.*

Right: *Bob Ray at the Italian International at San Remo in 1948.*

Motor Club

Bob Ray at the hill climb at Little Silver, Muddiford.

❧ Motor Club ☙

Left: *Bedford Drivers Club Rally on North Walk, 1936.*

Right: *A tug-of-war competition at the Bedford Drivers Club Rally on North Walk, 1936.*

Left: *The British team at the Austrian International in 1952. Bob is in the centre.*

Right: *Bob Harris is on the bike and Ron Woolaway is in the sidecar at trials at Beggars Roost near Lynmouth, late 1950s.*

❧ St John Ambulance ❧

The centenary celebrations of St John Ambulance Brigade in 1931, held in Rock Park.

Dedication of the St John Ambulance Brigade, 1937. Left to right, back row: H. Ward, L. Turner, ?, ?, ?, J. Furseman, A. Pester, J. Brayley, H. Curtis, P. Hurd, ?, ?; second row includes: Mrs Allway, R. Gerry, Mrs Pickering, Mrs Furseman, E. Isaac, Miss Shaddick, Mrs Knott, M. Curry. The men standing on left are, left to right: P. Heppenstall, Mr Latimer, Dr Forman, Mr F. Knott, Mr Pepperal, ?, ?. The Boys Cadets are: Sidney ?, S. Ackland, J. Featherstone, B. Gilbert, W. Turner, ? Turner, J. Hill, W. Cook, ?, H. Williams. The Girls Cadets are: ?, R. Spiller, ?, ?, A. Lashbrook, R. Tucker, C. Vanstone, H. Cyril, J. Corney, D. Pearson. The boys sitting are all unknown except Cyril Paul on the far left.

❧ St John Ambulance ❧

Left: *St John Ambulance Brigade Nursing Team, 1962/3.* Left to right: *Diane Down, Violet Mogridge, Nora Turner, Joyce Gorin, Patricia Lewis (Capt.).*

Below: *Princess Margaret meeting some of the St John Cadets after opening their new premises at Braddon House in 2000.* Left to right: *Deputy Area Commissioner Joanne Leathaby, Diane Arthur, Divisional Superintendent Joy Cann, Graham Braddon, Sheila Braddon, Jeremy and Angela Braddon.* The three children facing the camera: *Christopher and Alexandra Rendle and Natasha Connebear.* Photograph by Tony Freeman of Waverly Photographic.

Boy Scouts

Above: *1st North Devon Cub pack on parade along Taw Vale. Note Hopgoods Garage in the background, where today stands the Park Hotel.*

Above right: *1st North Devon Scout Group at the Junction Station, the date and occasion are unknown.* Photograph by kind permission of the *North Devon Journal Herald*.

The Cubs showing their skills at a demonstration in Rock Park, c.1954.

Left: *Scouts lending a helping hand at a fête at Pilton House in 1920.*

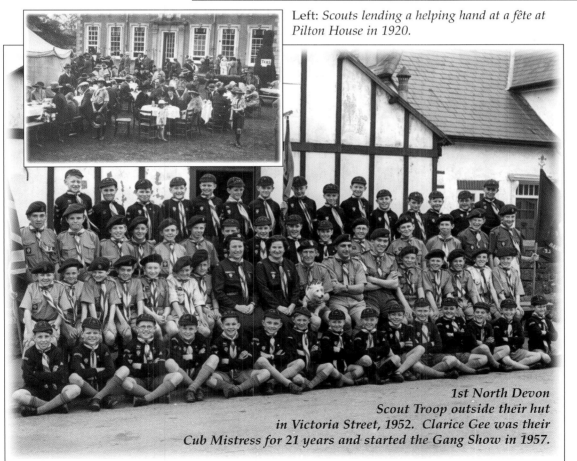

1st North Devon Scout Troop outside their hut in Victoria Street, 1952. Clarice Gee was their Cub Mistress for 21 years and started the Gang Show in 1957.

Girl Guides

Clarice Gee as a Girl Guide in 1935.

A Brownie meeting in the Cattle Market in the 1930s. The old prison in the background was where they held their meeting in an upstairs room.

Aerial view of Barnstaple's two bridges – ancient and modern – the new Western by-pass bridge seen here whilst under construction. Courtesy of North Devon Journal.

THE CHANGING FACE OF BARNSTAPLE

Many tides have ebbed and flowed under the bridge at Barnstaple since the Millennium and when the new down-stream bridge was built local drivers removed the 'Barnstaple – the home of the traffic jam' banners from their cars!

After years of deliberation, discussion and disagreements, digging began in February 2005 on what was to be the most momentous project in the first decade of this century.

This new Western by-pass joined the A39 Atlantic Highway near Newport and travelled to Pottington via 1.7 miles of new road, two roundabouts, three sets of traffic lights and a five-span bridge over the River Taw estuary. The project cost in the region of £42 million and opened on 23` May, 2007 in time for the Whitsun weekend traffic.

Since that day Barnstaple has sighed with relief, and although at rush hours the traffic slows down, gone are the teeth-grinding frustrations of drivers taking 'rat runs' through the back streets, which infuriated townspeople whether on wheels or not.

However, the by-pass did not come without certain criticism of the main round-about where Sticklepath Hill meets the new bridge. It was not the roundabout's design that caused the problem but what adorns it. Twelve clusters of huge slate slabs standing on end in metal cradles roused ire not only at the cost – *One of the set of Cornish slate clusters renamed locally as 'Barnhenge'.* £120,000 – but also because they came from Cornwall! Although the indignation has receded somewhat, the joke name of 'Barnhenge' has remained.

After the redesigning of the town's Square the area has become a Piazza where in fine weather you can enjoy the open space.

With the new bridge came a redesign of Barnstaple's Town Square. Away went the roundabout onto which vehicles entered from five directions and in came an easy-flowing route from the old bridge through to the relief road skirting the town.

The Square is now a Piazza where you can sit and enjoy the open space around the North Devon

The town celebrates in the Square in 2009 when the Christmas lights were turned on. The Town Management team arrange such musical events several times a year.

Museum. Here, also, townspeople and visitors join together and celebrate Christmas, New Year, the Carnival and other occasions. Taw Vale and The Strand are almost devoid of any traffic and a riverside walk from Rock Park to the Tarka Trail over the River Yeo can be a peaceful interlude with stunning views from Barnstaple's historic bridge along to its new counterpart.

Gone are the busy bus station, the trains trundling over the iron bridge with holidaymakers, airmen returning to their camp at Chivenor and the ships unloading their cargo at Castle Quay. Today you can breathe the unpolluted air and enjoy this historic area of the town.

Rebecca Brocklehurst, Education Outreach Worker seen here during the restoration work on the Albert Memorial Clock which was undertaken by the Town Council in 2009. A plaque marking the restoration has this delightful dedication to the inability of this timepiece to tell the same time on all four of its faces: "I tell the time, different each face, Adored, loved, pride of place".
C. Bater Courtesy of *North Devon Journal.*

What's in a Name?

Petroc. The word puzzled many of us when it appeared on road signs around the town in 2010. Might it be a new housing estate? Another superstore? But no. It was the new name of the North Devon College at the top of Old Sticklepath Hill.

Research tells me that in the 6th century St. Petroc ministered to the people of Devon, Cornwall and Somerset. Our Devon flag of green with a white cross is dedicated to him and so are 17 churches in the county.

It cost £330,000 to up-date and re-brand the ever-growing learning centre which when it opened in 1953 was the Barnstaple Technical College, known to all as, 'the Tech' - and still is to many of us! But Tech, College or PETROC – it's the achievements that count.

Barnstaple Traders

Few towns have not felt the cold winds of the world monetary recession in these early years of the 21st century, and Barnstaple is no exception. Earlier in this book we tell of the local traders whose families ran businesses for many generations, and recently whilst wandering around the town I decided to see how many of these still remain.

Established in 1835, the oldest business is removals firm Lewis & Sons who are still operating out of their original premises at Silver Street under sixth generation Simon Lewis. This is followed by Youings tobacconists and confectioners, now at the junction of High Street and Boutport Street and started by Frank Youings in 1884. Today great-grandson Peter Youings oversees the business from his wholesale warehouse at Barbican Close.

Sixth generation Simon Lewis (third from the left) *seen here with his father David and their removals team. Compare this photograph to the one on page 104.*

Where once stood wood merchants Rawle, Gammon and Baker on the banks of the River Yeo near Rolle Bridge there are now apartment blocks. The firm established in 1850 operates as a general builders merchant on the town's industrial estate at Pottington where it has easy access to the new downstream bridge and to the company's 14 other outlets in the West Country.

Other long-lived businesses include: County Garage, co-founded by James Squire in the 1920s and is managed by grandson Patrick Squire and great grandson Nicholas at their premises at Hollow Tree Road.

Department store Banburys opened in 1925 on the same site in the High Street and is managed by grandsons and great grandson of the original owner Arthur Banbury.

Padfields the furnishers, owned since the end of W.W.II by Kenneth Hooper is today run by grandson Jeremy Mills and his wife Elizabeth.

In the 1930s florist and fruiterer Smallridge was bought by Frank and Winifred James. The business in and around Holland Walk is today in the renowned floral hands of grandson Tony.

Once a trainee butcher in Butcher's Row, Percy Brend branched out into the hotel business in the 1960's. Today his family have built up an hospitality chain of 11 hotels and two restaurants which is reputed to be the biggest in the South West.

The end of the war saw Harold Badcock move to the town with his family and start his printing business which his grandson Stephen and grand daughter Michelle now run at their premises in Mill Road.

In 1956 Cyril and Joan Webber started their cycle shop in Bear Street. Today it sells prams and nursery equipment with grandson James holding the reins.

We must congratulate and support all the families who have formed and reformed their business into the 21st century. But what is sadly missed are our town centre bakers, butchers, ironmongers – so many that are mentioned earlier in this book. When friends get together and reminisce we speak of Trevisick's pies, Bromley's Tea Rooms and the wonderful cakes from Richard's the bakers. Butcher's Row, once full of butchers, today has just two!

Business rates, car parking charges, internet shopping and out of town supermarkets get the blame for the decline of the town centre. After all, who wouldn't want to park their car without charge and be able to purchase everything they require in one shopping outlet! Now, this is not a problem unique to our town but it is one that we have to address. How do we get the life blood running through the veins of this ancient borough of Barnstaple?

The Town Centre Management Team have been given the task of doing just that. This all-encompassing job co-ordinates business, security, functions, marketing, the police and councils and also events and celebrations in and around the town.

With the plans for a new college on Seven Brethren Bank, a shopping centre between Queen Street and Bear Street and a huge riverside redevelopment on Anchor Wood Bank all falling by the way side due to the economic downturn, the team had to find a way of improving and enhancing the potential of the town.

This took the form of a five year plan which was set in place in 2010 with the BID (Business Improvement District) Barnstaple scheme. Eye-catching, television advertising, a colourful brochure highlighting shopping, leisure and cultural activities and an investment of £700,000 back the vision of, "a vibrant, welcoming and prosperous town centre that cherishes its rich history, encourages innovation and aims to be one of the primary retail and business destinations in the South West".

Events Held in the Town

Thousands of people lined the streets of Barnstaple in April 2009 to welcome home 600 of the Commando Logistics Regiment based at RMB Chivenor. They had just returned from a tough six months tour in Helmand Province, Afghanistan. School children were excused lessons and shops shut while people cheered on the troops in celebration of their safe return although there was sadness at the loss of two of their colleagues Cpl. Rob Deering and Mne Damian Davies. After a further tour in Afghanistan the Royal Marines from Chivenor received the Freedom on the Borough in November 2011. Courtesy of *North Devon Journal.*

The dancing ladies of the 2009 Greenman Festival which takes place each year in Pilton Street. Courtesy of *North Devon Journal.*

Barnstaple's own Grand Prix held between The Strand and the old Barnstaple Town Station was a roaring success in May 2012.

When the Olympic torch arrived in Roundswell, Barnstaple on the 21 May 2012 the first torch bearer was Fremington Parish and District Councillor Frank Biederman.

Barnstaple meets Barnstable

Twinning with towns abroad has given Barnstaple people – especially the youngsters – a look at the day-to-day lives of our counterparts in France, Germany, Italy and America.

Our nearest twin is the French coastal town of Trouville-sur-Mer which we linked with in 1975. The Allied Forces stationed in Germany opened a post-war door for links with Stadt Uelzen which became official in 1967, and particularly popular over the years have been the concerts given by the town bands during exchange visits. With all our twinning there is warm hospitality on both sides, not least in the latest links forged with historic Italian town of Susa.

The first of all our overseas 'family' ties - and furthest away – is our namesake Barnstable in Massachusetts.

Since 1939, when Barnstaple's Mayor Charles Dart visited our sister town in the USA, there have been many exchange visits of town dignitaries between Barnstaple, Devon and Barnstable, Massachusetts.

Most of the visits to Barnstable have been organised, co-ordinated and chaperoned by Louis Cataldo who was Chief of Police and Deputy Sheriff of Barnstable County. (Confusingly, on Cape Cod there is Barnstable Village, Town and County!)

Louis Cataldo who was made a burgess of Barnstaple in appreciation of his many years of co-ordinating the twinning of our town of Barnstaple and his town of Barnstable in the USA.

Louis is also a respected historian who has recorded and written the memories of Cape Codders down through the years and is now in the process of installing all his work in a museum dedicated to it. He has visited Barnstaple and has a great affinity for our town, its people and its history, and keeps in contact with many friends he has made during twinning visits.

In 2004 I accepted an invitation to visit Barnstable where Louis Cataldo asked me to give a talk about Barnstaple. I experienced at first hand the warm hospitality of Louis and his wife Lora who took time to introduce me to the Town Manager, the County Commissioners, the offices and staff of the local newspaper, *Cape Cod Patriot*, the Law Courts and JFK Library. I was guest on a television chat show (seen by 100,000 viewers!) and came home not only bearing gifts but with an immense impression of how

popular Louis was among his people and how much time and work he has put into promoting the ties between our communities.

In 2005 Louis was made a burgess of Barnstaple – a rare and ancient honour and the highest tribute our town could pay him for half a century of unique friendship.

Sport and the Arts

Obesity is seen as a major health threat to our population and especially to our children. But here in Barnstaple our young people along with their elders are far more aware of their fitness than a decade ago. Cyclists, joggers and walkers are a common sight on our roads and along the Tarka Trail from Braunton to Barnstaple and on to Bideford. In fact, many use the Trail to cycle to work. This cuts down on fuel consumption and keeps up the fitness!

Barnstaple's schools are to be praised for their sporting facilities. The Leisure Centre built in 1975 on the banks of the River Taw has proved to be a great incentive with its, gym, indoor bowls, racquet sports, exercise classes and refurbished swimming pool in great demand.

Another feather in the town's cap was the opening in 2003 of the Tarka Tennis arena which cost £4.5 million. It has six indoor and four outdoor courts and a packed programme of classes and events. This includes the prestigious Aegon GB Pro Series which sees top seeded women players competing. The club also holds Pilate classes, has a running club and football academy and an Outreach programme that takes tennis to primary and secondary schools in the area. A £1million hall next to the Tarka arena will house the Falcons Gymnastics Academy. The original Club started at Pottington Estate in 2004 with a membership of 75 children and now has 550 gymnasts who take part from recreational level to those who compete at national events. The club is especially

Mahesh Shah puts the final touches to the Tarka Tennis Centre before it opened in 2003.
Courtesy of *North Devon Journal.*

Gymnasts and instructors of the Falcons Gymnastic Academy who will soon be moving into their purpose built hall alongside the Tarka Tennis Centre.

proud of Adam Tobin and Joe Jones who have been chosen for the national squad.

Splashing about on the river is just what the town's newest sporting club does at every opportunity. The Barnstaple Pilot Gig Club was founded in January 2010 and within 12 months they had 50 keen rowing members who can be seen training hard on the River Taw in preparation for the many regattas in the South West.

With a large donation from the Keith Abraham's Charitable Trust in 2011 the club was able to have a race gig built and within weeks the *Lady Freda* and her team were competing in the World Pilot Gig Championships on the Isles of Scilly. They were back again this year with four crews participating in all aspects of the championships and returning to Barnstaple with results to be proud of.

North Devon Theatres' Trust

This year is not only the Diamond Jubilee of Queen Elizabeth II but also of our own Queen's Theatre. The interior of the hall had been badly damaged by fire during W.W.II and the council decided to restore the building to celebrate The Festival of Britain. It was reopened in 1952. The Queen and the Duke of Edinburgh visited it when they came to Barnstaple in May 1956.

As the Queen's Hall it had been the home of dance, drama, music, political meetings, antique fairs, banquets, flower and dog shows and many other social occasions. Its heydays were between the 1950s and 1980s and then gradually it lost its sparkle. The big name bands which had been happy to play here found bigger and better venues to beat their drums, although the local amateur thespians were only too happy to continue entertaining their audiences. However, with finances at rock bottom the Council decided to shut up shop in 1993 and refurbish and update the theatre.

When Alan Giddings came to town as the Chief Executive of the new Queen's Theatre Trust, a registered charity, he had a tough job to lift the theatre out of its financial doldrums. But this he did!

With Alan's guidance and foresight the theatre has gone from the mediocre to the spectacular where premier bands and orchestras play and famous comedians raise a laugh. World renowned ballet, opera and theatre companies are well received, along with continued strong support for amateur dramatic and musical societies and, of course, the Gang Show.

The North Devon Festival, first held in 1999, was instigated by North Devon Council who asked local people to suggest a programme of events. Alan Dodd was then the co-ordinator, building and shaping it to huge success over the years. The festival which was held throughout June encompassed art, drama, literature and sport - in fact, anything and everything that would entertain, amuse and thrill.

Street artists in the town centre showed their skills with juggling, escapology and acrobatics. There were exhibitions of paintings, sculpture and photography, and music of all kinds including a jazz band playing on the Tarka Music Train as it journeyed between Barnstaple and Exmouth and a group from Zimbabwe who performed a gumboot dance.

In 2004 we celebrated the 150th anniversary of the railway coming to the town, and a year later we marked the 150th year of the Pannier Market with traders in Victorian costume selling their wares from pannier baskets.

In 2012, along with other regions, our funding for arts projects has been drastically cut and therefore the North Devon Festival cannot take its full form as in previous years. However, it will carry on with three key aspects – a four day Drama Festival in June with 32 companies in a mini Edinburgh Festival at venues around the town; Art Trek in July, where 100 artists open their homes for visitors to view their work; and the Barnstaple Fringe in October and April, with performances in pubs and restau-

The launch of North Devon Festival in 2005 outside the Queen's Theatre, Barnstaple.

rants and mostly free to their customers! So we may be losing the month-long festival with all its diversity, but could gain from a wider time-spread of events.

Festival Administrator Claire Thompson, said they have to thank the North Devon Council for supporting them as much as they can in this time of financial constraint, and the aim is to continue to provide arts and culture for local people and for the benefit of tourism in North Devon.

Barnstaple Celebrates Queen Elizabeth II Diamond Jubilee

The first weekend of June 2012 was dedicated to the 60 years reign of Queen Elizabeth II but like her Coronation on 2 June 1953 it was met by dismal weather conditions. However, the country came together and celebrated, and Barnstaple was no exception.

From street parties to the Picnic in the Park, from garden barbecues to village hall fêtes and even a Real Ale Festival, we all found a way of marking the occasion.